Baking
with kids

Baking
with kids

LINDA COLLISTER
photography by Polly Wreford

RYLAND
PETERS
& SMALL

LONDON NEW YORK

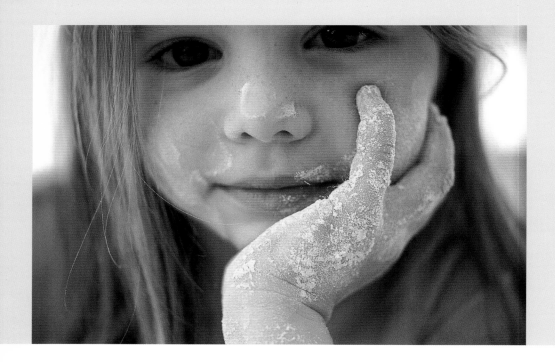

Senior Designer Megan Smith
Commissioning Editor Julia Charles
Production Gemma Moules
Art Director Anne-Marie Bulat
Publishing Director Alison Starling

Food Stylist Joss Herd
Stylist Helen Trent
Indexer Hilary Bird

First published in Great Britain in 2006
by Ryland Peters & Small
20–21 Jockey's Fields
London WC1R 4BW
www.rylandpeters.com

10 9 8 7 6 5 4 3 2 1

Text © Linda Collister 2006
Design and photographs
© Ryland Peters & Small 2006

Printed in China

ISBN-13: 978 1 84597 219 6
ISBN-10: 1 84597 219 8

A CIP record for this book is available
from the British Library.

Author's acknowledgements
I would like to thank the following for their help
with this book: Barbara Levy, Julia Charles, Megan
Smith, Gemma Moules, Polly Wreford, Joss Herd,
Helen Trent, Dan, Stevie and Emily Hertz and, last
but not least, all of the delightful children featured
in the photographs.

Notes
All spoon measurements are level unless otherwise
specified. All eggs are UK large size, unless
otherwise specified. Uncooked or partly cooked
eggs should not be served to the very young, the
very old, those with compromised immune systems
or to pregnant women.

Ovens should be preheated to the specified
temperatures. All ovens work slightly differently. We
recommend using an oven thermometer and
suggest you consult the maker's handbook for any
special instructions – particularly if you are using a
fan-assisted oven as you may need to adjust
cooking temperatures.

*To Elsa Petersen-Schepelern
(1948–2005) who was
responsible for the birth of
this book.*

contents

introduction

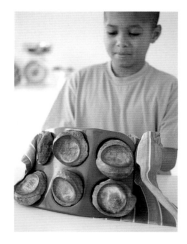

Baking is irresistible to any child: you turn a bag of flour, a box of eggs, a heap of sugar and a brick of butter into a cake! Call it magic, chemistry or just a chance to lick the icing bowl – it's great fun. Cooking and eating together is a delightful part of family life and a vital part of a child's education. It's a fun way to learn – not just about food and nutrition, but also about planning, co-operation, organization and patience.

So, at what age should you get the kids involved? Our children started by mixing bowls of pancake batter at 18 months. They came with us to farmers' markets and to fishmonger's and butcher's shops and helped to plan and shop for meals. Two-year-olds love playing with a piece of dough. At three they can be making cookies, shaping bread rolls and decorating cupcakes. Our children are older now, but they still like playing with dough; if it is too wet for football after school they bring their friends in to make fresh pasta noodles!

Each of my children still picks the supper menu one night a week and helps with preparation. We grow tomatoes, strawberries, plums and herbs in tubs on our patio garden. The children feel a great sense of achievement when eating what they have produced. We talk about how good fruit and vegetables taste, about the difference in flavour between apple varieties, about which of our tomatoes works best in a simple salad and about how important they are for our health.

In the kitchen you need some ground rules so that your children quickly get into a habit of hygiene and safety. Wash hands, pull up long sleeves, avoid dangly jewellery and fussy clothes, tie back long hair and wear an apron. It may just be common sense, but explaining the reasons behind the rules helps! Make sure they understand that kitchen knives and other equipment are not toys and must be treated carefully. You should also explain that the oven can get very hot so they should keep their distance and why chopping boards, work surfaces and washing-up cloths must be kept very clean. It's most important that everyone washes their hands and any chopping boards and knives really well with plenty of soap and hot water after handling raw chicken or meat, and that these foods are kept, and stored, separate from other ingredients.

Read the recipe through with your child before you start so that you both know what you are doing. Decide which parts of the recipe your child can safely manage; you know their abilities best; then get out all the equipment and ingredients and work together. If possible invest in a few pieces of good-quality, child-friendly equipment such as non-stick baking trays, a roasting tin, bowls with non-slip rubber bases, a rotary whisk, some short-handled wooden spoons, a bowl scraper, a safe cheese grater, a kitchen timer and oven gloves. Older children with cooking experience can usually take a cake out of the oven without assistance, but straining a pan full of boiling pasta is always best done by an adult. NEVER leave a child under 10 alone in the kitchen to cook or use the microwave without adult supervision.

Accept that there will be a lot of clearing up, but give each child a specific task, such as sweeping the floor, rather than a long list of duties. Why not put on some favourite sing-along music!

Cooking is fun, brings a huge sense of achievement, and – of course – something wonderful to eat. Happy baking!

teatime favourites

Apple crumble is one of our favourite family desserts. We came up with this tasty muffin so that we could enjoy the lovely, crumbly topping and fresh appley taste at teatime as well as after dinner. You could also pop one in your lunchbox.

apple crumble muffins

Makes 12 muffins

For the topping:
50 g unsalted butter, chilled
50 g Demerara sugar (or
    caster sugar)
50 g plain flour
50 g ground almonds
    (optional)

For the base:
275 g plain flour
2 teaspoons baking powder
175 g caster sugar
1 unwaxed lemon
150 g unsalted butter
2 large free-range eggs
100 ml milk
2 medium eating apples,
    washed

*a 12-hole muffin tray lined
    with paper muffin cases*

1 ASK AN ADULT TO HELP YOU preheat the oven to 190°C (375°F) Gas 5.

2 Make the topping first. Cut the butter into small pieces and put it into a mixing bowl with the sugar, flour and ground almonds. Work the ingredients together until they look like small peas. Put on one side until needed.

3 Set a large sieve over a mixing bowl. Tip the flour into the sieve. Measure the baking powder into the sieve then sift into the bowl. Add the sugar to the bowl and mix in with a wooden spoon.

4 Carefully grate the yellow zest from the lemon (or use a special citrus zester) leaving the white pith on the fruit. Add to the bowl and stir in. Make a well in the centre of the ingredients.

5 ASK AN ADULT TO HELP YOU carefully melt the butter in a small pan over low heat, or you can melt it in the microwave. Pour into the well.

6 Break the eggs into a small bowl. Pick out any pieces of shell, then beat the eggs with a fork just to break up the yolks. Tip into the well in the mixing bowl then pour in the milk. Mix gently with a wooden spoon.

7 Spoon the mixture into the paper muffin cases, making sure there is the same amount in each.

8 Carefully cut each apple into quarters, then cut out the core. Roughly chop the apples. Scatter the apple pieces on top of the muffin mixture. Sprinkle the topping over the apples.

9 ASK AN ADULT TO HELP YOU put the muffins in the preheated oven to bake for 30 minutes, until golden brown. ASK AN ADULT TO HELP YOU carefully remove the tray from the oven and leave to cool for 2 minutes. Transfer the muffins to a wire rack and leave to cool completely. Store your muffins in an airtight container and eat them within 3 days.

Scones are a traditional teatime treat. They are a cross between bread and cake. Eat them cut in two and spread with butter and jam or some honey. A traditional 'cream tea' in a teashop is scones spread with strawberry jam and thick clotted cream. You can flavour your scones with sultanas and raisins if you like, or leave out the sugar and add some grated Cheddar cheese with a big pinch of cayenne pepper.

scones

Makes about 8 scones

Basic recipe:
250 g plain flour
4 teaspoons baking powder
a good pinch of salt
50 g caster sugar
50 g unsalted butter, at room
    temperature, plus a little
    extra for greasing
1 large free-range egg
about 100 ml milk

a non-stick baking tray
a round biscuit cutter, about
    6.5 cm or a drinking glass
    of the same diameter

1 ASK AN ADULT TO HELP YOU preheat the oven to 220°C (425°F) Gas 7. Put a little butter on a piece of kitchen paper and rub it over the baking tray to lightly grease it.

2 Set a sieve over a mixing bowl. Tip the flour, baking powder, salt and sugar into it and sift into the bowl. Using an ordinary round-bladed table knife, cut up the butter into tiny pieces and add to the bowl.

3 Toss the pieces of butter in the flour so they are well coated, then rub the butter into the flour – to do this, pick up a handful of the mixture with your fingers, then rub the mixture between the very ends of your fingers so the bits of butter become smaller and smaller as they mix with the flour. Keep rubbing in until the whole mixture looks like crumbs. Make a hollow in the centre of the crumby mixture.

4 Break the egg into a measuring jug. Mix with a fork just to break up the yolk and the white then pour in enough milk to make up the mixture to 150 ml.

5 Pour three-quarters of the milk mixture into the hollow. Using the table knife, stir the liquid and the flour mixture together to make a soft, coarse-looking dough. If the dough is dry and crumbly and won't stick together, stir in more of the milk mixture a tablespoon at a time.

6 Tip out the dough onto a work surface lightly covered with flour. Work and knead the ball of dough with your hands for a few seconds so it looks smoother. Dip your hands in a little more flour then pat out the dough until it is about 3 cm thick. Dip the cutter in flour then cut out rounds. Gather up the scraps into a ball, then press out and cut out more rounds.

7 Put all the rounds onto the prepared baking tray, setting them slightly apart. ASK AN ADULT TO HELP YOU put the tray in the preheated oven to bake for 12 to 15 minutes, until golden brown. ASK AN ADULT TO HELP YOU remove the tray from the oven and set it on a heatproof surface. Transfer the scones to a wire rack using a metal spatula or fish slice. Your scones are best eaten the same day and are also good toasted.

This is a really quick and easy recipe. The buns are packed with a mixture of dried fruit – cherries, cranberries, strawberries and blueberries. You'll find bags of these mixed dried 'berries and cherries' in supermarkets and wholefood stores, or you can also use jumbo raisins and sultanas. Why not make up your own combination?

cherry berry buns

Makes 18 small buns

250 g plain flour
4 teaspoons baking powder
¼ teaspoon ground mixed spice
100 g unsalted butter, at room temperature
50 g light brown muscovado sugar
125 g cherry berry mix (see above)
1 large free-range egg
4–5 tablespoons milk
caster or demerara sugar, for sprinkling

2 non-stick baking trays, lightly greased

1 ASK AN ADULT TO HELP YOU preheat the oven to 200°C (400°F) Gas 6.

2 Set a large sieve over a mixing bowl. Tip the flour into the sieve. Add the baking powder and mixed spice to the sieve and sift these ingredients into the bowl.

3 Cut the butter into small pieces and add to the bowl. Work the butter into the flour by rubbing it in with the tips of your fingers – to do this pick up some of the mixture with just the ends of your fingers and thumb, then rub your fingers and thumb together so the butter pieces get smaller and smaller and gradually disappear so that the mixture looks like breadcrumbs.

4 Stir in the muscovado sugar and cherry berry mix and make a well in the mixture.

5 Break the egg into a small bowl. Pick out any pieces of shell, then add 4 tablespoons of milk and beat the mixture with a fork just to break up the egg and mix it with the milk.

6 Pour into the well in the flour mixture. Mix all the ingredients together with a round-bladed knife to make a firm dough. If there are dry crumbs or the dough won't mix together add another tablespoon of milk.

7 Drop spoonfuls of the mixture on to the prepared trays, using about a heaped tablespoon of mixture for each bun, spacing them slightly apart. Sprinkle each bun with a little caster sugar.

8 ASK AN ADULT TO HELP YOU put the buns in the preheated oven to bake for 15 minutes, until golden brown. ASK AN ADULT TO HELP YOU remove the trays from the oven and leave to cool for 2 minutes. Transfer the buns to a wire rack to cool completely. Store your buns in an airtight container and eat them within 3 days.

Here is something you can do on a rainy day. Bake some cupcakes and decorate them with a fudgy topping and some jelly beans or anything you like – try chocolate buttons, dolly mixtures or hundreds and thousands.

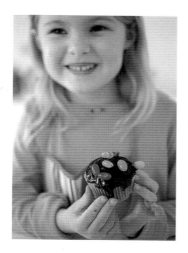

chocolate cupcakes

Makes 12 cupcakes

For the cakes:
6oz **175 g plain flour**
1 teaspoon baking powder
a pinch of salt
1oz **25 g cocoa powder**
5oz **150 g caster sugar**
4oz **100 g unsalted butter,
     very soft**
2 large free-range eggs
¼pt **125 ml milk**

For the topping:
4oz **100 g plain chocolate**
1 tablespoon golden syrup
1oz **25 g unsalted butter**

*a 12-hole muffin tray lined
with paper muffin cases*

1 ASK AN ADULT TO HELP YOU preheat the oven to 180°C (350°F) Gas 4.

2 Place a large sieve over a mixing bowl. Tip the flour, baking powder, salt, cocoa powder and sugar into the sieve as you measure them, then sift into the bowl.

3 Add the very soft butter to the bowl. Break the eggs into a small bowl, pick out any pieces of shell then beat the eggs with a fork until they are a bit frothy.

4 Pour the eggs and milk into the bowl. Use a wooden spoon to mix all the ingredients together to make a smooth cake batter.

5 Carefully spoon the cake mixture into the paper cases, putting an equal amount into each one.

6 ASK AN ADULT TO HELP YOU put the cakes in the preheated oven to bake for 20 minutes, until just firm to the touch. ASK AN ADULT TO HELP YOU remove the tray from the oven and leave to cool for about 2 minutes. Transfer the cupcakes to a wire rack and leave to cool completely.

7 While the cakes are cooling, make the topping. Break up the chocolate and put it in a small heatproof bowl with the golden syrup and butter. ASK AN ADULT TO HELP YOU place the bowl over a saucepan filled with steaming hot but not boiling water. Stir gently with a wooden spoon until smooth and melted. Remove the bowl from the pan. Leave to cool for 5 minutes.

8 To finish the cakes, spoon the smooth runny chocolate topping on top of the cakes and add your decoration. Leave it to set before eating. Store your cupcakes in an airtight container and eat them within 4 days.

These lovely chewy bars are made with a basic mixture of butter, honey, sugar, oats, flour and baking powder. You can add your own favourite dried fruits, seeds and nuts or you could replace the nuts with chopped dates, dried figs or dried cranberries. Use my recipe below as a starting point and experiment to find out what you like best to create your own special version.

muesli bars

Makes 16 bars

100 g unsalted butter
130 g clear honey
2 tablespoons light brown
   muscovado sugar
300 g porridge oats
2 tablespoons plain flour
½ teaspoon baking powder
50 g ready-to-eat dried
   apricots, chopped
2 tablespoons sunflower
   seeds
2 tablespoons sesame seeds
2 tablespoons raisins
100 g mixed nuts or dried fruit
   and nut mix, chopped

*20.5 x 28 cm brownie or
   tray-bake tin*
*non-stick baking parchment
   or greaseproof paper*

1 ASK AN ADULT TO HELP YOU preheat the oven to 160°C (325°F) Gas 3. Grease the inside of the tin with a small amount of very soft butter on a piece of kitchen paper. Cut a rectangle from a sheet of non-stick baking parchment or greaseproof paper the same size as the tin, and fit it into the bottom of the tin.

2 Put the butter in a large saucepan. Add the honey and sugar. ASK AN ADULT TO HELP YOU put the pan over low heat. Heat gently until the butter melts. Carefully remove the pan from the heat. Stir gently with a wooden spoon. Tip all the rest of the ingredients into the pan and stir well with the wooden spoon.

3 Transfer the mixture to the prepared tin and spread evenly. Press the mixture into the tin with the back of a spoon.

4 ASK AN ADULT TO HELP YOU put the tin in the preheated oven to bake for 30 minutes, until golden brown. ASK AN ADULT TO HELP YOU remove the tin from the oven and put it on a wire rack. Leave it to cool completely.

5 Loosen the mixture from the tin by running a round-bladed knife inside the edge of the tin, then flip the tin upside down onto a cutting board so the muesli mixture falls out in one piece. Cut it into 16 bars. Store your bars in an airtight container and eat them within a week.

This easy recipe makes crunchy biscuits that are perfect to eat with a glass of milk when you get home from school. The ginger is what makes them spicy and the black treacle gives them a lovely toffee flavour.

ginger snaps

Makes 24 biscuits

350 g plain flour
1 teaspoon bicarbonate
of soda
3 teaspoons baking powder
3 teaspoons ground ginger
1 teaspoon ground cinnamon
200 g caster sugar, plus extra
for sprinkling
115 g unsalted butter
85 g black treacle
1 large free-range egg

2 non-stick baking trays

1 ASK AN ADULT TO HELP YOU preheat the oven to 160°C (325°F) Gas 3. Grease the baking trays with soft butter, using a piece of kitchen paper.

2 Set a sieve over a large bowl. Tip the flour, bicarbonate of soda, baking powder, ground ginger and cinnamon into the sieve and sift into the bowl. Add the sugar and mix in with a wooden spoon. Make a hollow in the middle of the flour mixture.

3 Put the butter and treacle in a small saucepan. ASK AN ADULT TO HELP YOU melt the butter and treacle gently over very low heat – warm the pan just enough to melt the ingredients, don't let the mixture become hot.

4 Carefully pour the melted mixture into the hollow in the flour.

5 Break the egg into a small bowl, remove any pieces of shell and break it up with a fork.

6 Pour the egg into the hollow on top of the melted mixture. Mix all the ingredients together with a wooden spoon. As soon as the dough starts to come together put your hands into the bowl and start to push the warm dough together. If the dough feels a bit too warm wait for it to cool.

7 When the dough has come together use your hands to roll it into 24 balls, slightly smaller than table tennis balls, but larger than big marbles.

8 Arrange well apart on the prepared baking trays then flatten the balls with your fingers. Sprinkle them with a little sugar.

9 ASK AN ADULT TO HELP YOU put the biscuits in the preheated oven to bake for about 15 minutes, until lightly browned around the edges.

10 ASK AN ADULT TO HELP YOU remove the trays from the oven. Leave them on a heatproof work surface to cool for 5 minutes. When the biscuits feel firm enough to move, gently lift them on to a wire rack using a large metal spatula or fish slice. Let them cool completely. Store your biscuits in an airtight container and eat them within 5 days.

christmas spice cookies

Makes about 24 cookies

300 g plain flour

2 teaspoons ground cinnamon

½ teaspoon ground ginger

½ teaspoon ground mixed spice

175 g unsalted butter, straight from the fridge, plus extra butter for greasing

6 tablespoons clear honey

thin ribbon, thread or raffia, to hang

writing icing pens and silver balls, to decorate

a selection of shaped cookie cutters such as stars, Christmas trees, angels, bells and reindeer

2 non-stick baking trays

1 Put a little bit of butter on a small piece of kitchen paper and rub it over the baking trays to lightly grease them.

2 Put the flour, cinnamon, ginger and mixed spice in the bowl of a food processor. Using an ordinary table knife, cut the butter into small pieces and add to the bowl of the processor.

3 ASK AN ADULT TO HELP YOU run the processor until the mixture looks like fine crumbs.

4 Measure the honey into the bowl of the processor and WITH ADULT HELP run the processor until the mixture comes together to make a ball of dough.

5 ASK AN ADULT TO HELP YOU remove the blade from the bowl, then remove the dough from the bowl. Wrap the dough in cling film or greaseproof paper and put it into the fridge until it is firm enough to roll out – about 30 minutes.

6 ASK AN ADULT TO HELP YOU preheat the oven to 180°C (350°F) Gas 4.

7 Sprinkle the work surface and a rolling pin with flour. Gently roll out the dough until it is about 5 mm thick. Cut out shapes using your cutters. Gather up the trimmings into a ball then roll out and cut more shapes. To make Christmas decorations you can hang up you'll need to make a small hole at the top of each cookie with a cocktail stick (make sure the hole is large enough to thread a ribbon through).

8 Arrange the shapes slightly apart on the baking trays. ASK AN ADULT TO HELP YOU put them in the oven to bake for about 10 minutes, or until golden. ASK AN ADULT TO HELP YOU carefully remove from the oven and put the trays onto a heatproof surface and leave to cool for 5 minutes. Gently transfer the cookies to a wire rack and leave until cold.

9 Decorate however you like: thread them with ribbon then ice using coloured icing pens and silver balls. Leave until set then hang up. Eat your cookies as soon as possible or store them in an airtight container and eat within 5 days.

It's fun to make your own edible Christmas decorations or treats for a special birthday party. You cut shapes out of a sweet biscuit dough and have lots of fun decorating them with coloured icing and silver balls.

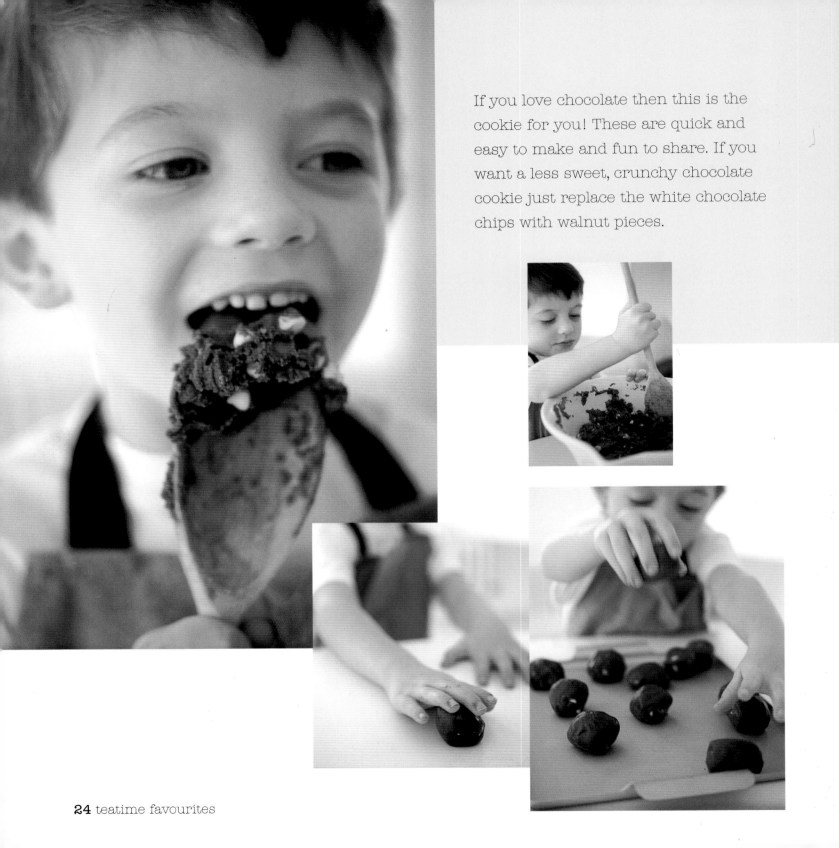

If you love chocolate then this is the cookie for you! These are quick and easy to make and fun to share. If you want a less sweet, crunchy chocolate cookie just replace the white chocolate chips with walnut pieces.

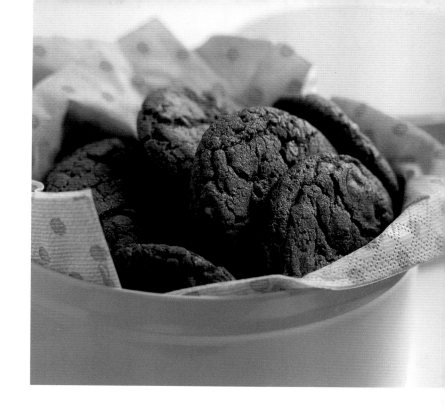

triple choc cookies

Makes 24 cookies

125 g unsalted butter, at room temperature
100 g caster sugar
100 g light brown muscovado sugar
1 large free-range egg
225 g plain flour
2½ tablespoons cocoa powder
½ teaspoon baking powder
½ teaspoon bicarbonate of soda
a pinch of salt
100 g plain chocolate chips
100 g white chocolate chips

2–3 non-stick baking trays, ungreased

1 ASK AN ADULT TO HELP YOU preheat the oven to 180°C (350°F) Gas 4.

2 Put the soft butter in a mixing bowl or the bowl of an electric mixer. Add the caster sugar and brown sugar and beat with a wooden spoon or the whisk attachment until the mixture looks very soft and fluffy. Scrape down the sides of the bowl with a plastic scraper every now and then so all the ingredients get fully beaten up.

3 Break the egg into a small bowl. Remove any pieces of shell then break up the egg with a fork. Add the egg to the mixing bowl and beat the mixture well.

4 Set a sieve over the mixing bowl. Tip the flour, cocoa powder, baking powder, bicarbonate of soda and salt into the sieve then sift these ingredients into the bowl. Mix in with the wooden spoon, or with the electric mixer on low speed.

5 Add all the chocolate chips to the bowl and mix in with a wooden spoon until everything is thoroughly combined.

6 To make the mixture into cookies, dip your hands in cold water so they are just damp then take a small amount of the mixture – about a rounded tablespoon – and roll it into a ball. Set the ball on to the prepared baking tray, then make 23 more balls in the same way. Set the balls about 3 cm apart on the trays.

7 ASK AN ADULT TO HELP YOU put the cookies in the preheated oven to bake for 15 minutes. ASK AN ADULT TO HELP YOU carefully remove the trays from the oven and leave to cool for 5 minutes before transferring the cookies to a wire rack. Leave to cool completely, then store in an airtight container. Eat your cookies within a week of baking them.

These irresistible cookies are made with the same oats that you eat at breakfast time. Why not make a box for the next 'bring and buy' sale at school? You can add dried fruit like jumbo raisins or dried cherries and cranberries, chopped nuts, or even choc chips.

oatie cookies

Makes 18 cookies

125 g unsalted butter, plus extra for greasing

100 g caster sugar

100 g dark brown muscovado sugar

1 large free-range egg

150 g porridge oats

125 g plain flour

a pinch of salt

¼ teaspoon bicarbonate of soda

½ teaspoon vanilla essence

75 g raisins, dried cherries, dried cranberries, chopped nuts or chocolate chips

2 non-stick baking trays

1 ASK AN ADULT TO HELP YOU preheat the oven to 180°C (350°F) Gas 4. Put a little soft butter on a piece of kitchen paper and rub it over the baking trays so they are greased.

2 Put the butter in a saucepan that's big enough to hold all the ingredients. ASK AN ADULT TO HELP YOU melt the butter over low heat. Remove the pan from the heat and put it on a heatproof work surface. Tip both the sugars into the pan and mix into the butter with a wooden spoon. Make sure you stir until all the lumps of sugar have been broken up.

3 Break the egg into a small bowl. Pick out any pieces of shell and lightly beat the egg with a fork just to break it up. Pour the egg into the pan and mix it in.

4 Add the porridge oats to the pan and stir well. Add the flour, salt, bicarbonate of soda and vanilla essence and mix well.

5 Finally add your choice of dried fruit, nuts or chocolate and mix until thoroughly combined.

6 Using a rounded tablespoon of mixture for each cookie, drop the mixture onto the trays making sure they are well apart. Gently flatten the mounds of dough with your fingers. ASK AN ADULT TO HELP YOU put the cookies in the preheated oven to bake for 13 to 15 minutes, until lightly browned. ASK AN ADULT TO HELP YOU remove the trays from the oven. Leave to cool for 2 minutes then use a metal spatula to lift the cookies off the trays and onto a wire rack to cool completely. Store your cookies in an airtight container and eat them within 5 days.

Popovers are a sort of puffy, muffin-sized roll with a crisp brown crust and a hollow, moist inside. The name is said to come from the fact that as the batter bakes it expands and 'pops over' the sides of the cups in the baking tin. You can eat them straight from the oven with maple syrup or honey and a knob of butter. The batter takes seconds to make in a food processor so why not try them for breakfast at the weekend or as a delicious after-school snack?

popovers

Makes 12 popovers

250 ml milk
125 g plain flour
¼ teaspoon salt
1 tablespoon wheatgerm or
   oat bran
3 large free-range eggs
25 g unsalted butter, or 2
   tablespoons melted butter,
   plus extra for greasing the
   moulds

a 12-hole muffin tray or
   flexible moulds set on a
   baking tray

1 ASK AN ADULT TO HELP YOU preheat the oven to 220°C (425°F) Gas 7. Put a little butter on a piece of kitchen paper and rub it inside the holes of the muffin tray so they are lightly greased.

2 Put the milk, flour, salt and wheatgerm or oat bran into the bowl of a food processor or blender.

3 Break the eggs into a small bowl, pick out any pieces of shell then pour the eggs into the processor or blender.

4 ASK AN ADULT TO HELP YOU melt the butter in a small pan over low heat, or in the microwave. Pour the melted butter into the processor or blender. Put the lid on tightly and WITH ADULT HELP run the processor or blender for about 20 seconds or until you have a smooth batter.

5 ASK AN ADULT TO HELP YOU remove the processor blade, then pour the batter into a jug. If you have a blender that pours you don't need to do this. Pour the batter into the 12 holes of the muffin tray, or into the flexible moulds, so that each one is about half-filled.

6 ASK AN ADULT TO HELP YOU put the popovers in the preheated oven to bake for 25 minutes. Then, without opening the oven door, turn down the heat to 180°C (350°F) Gas 4 and bake for another 15 minutes. ASK AN ADULT TO HELP YOU remove the popovers from the oven and tip them out of the muffin tray or moulds onto a serving plate. Eat your popovers straightaway while they are still warm from the oven.

This loaf makes a tasty teatime snack. Cut it into thick slices and either eat it plain or spread it with cream cheese or hazelnut and chocolate spread. It's even good toasted! You will need to use really ripe bananas.

banana loaf

Makes 1 medium loaf cake

250 g plain flour
1 teaspoon baking powder
a good pinch of salt
75 g light brown muscovado
   sugar
75 g caster sugar
100 g unsalted butter, plus
   extra for greasing tin
2 large free-range eggs
250 g peeled ripe bananas –
   about 2 large bananas
75 g plain chocolate chips or
   chunks

a 900 g loaf tin
greaseproof paper or non-
   stick baking parchment

1 ASK AN ADULT TO HELP YOU preheat the oven to 180°C (350°F) Gas 4. Put a small amount of soft butter on a piece of kitchen paper and rub it around the inside of the tin so it is coated in a thin layer of grease. Cut a strip of greaseproof paper or non-stick baking parchment the same width as the tin and as long as the base plus the height of each end of the tin. Fit the paper into the tin so it covers the base and the two short ends of the tin.

2 Put the flour, baking powder and salt into a sieve set over a mixing bowl and sift into the bowl. Add the sugars and stir in with a wooden spoon. Make a well in the centre.

3 Put the butter into a small pan. ASK AN ADULT TO HELP YOU melt the butter over very low heat or do it in the microwave. Break the eggs into a small bowl and pick out any pieces of shell. Beat the eggs with a fork just to break them up.

4 Add the melted butter and the eggs to the well in the flour mixture.

5 Put the peeled bananas on to a plate and mash with a fork, but don't make them too smooth or like a purée – there should still be some lumpy bits.

6 Add the bananas and chocolate chips to the well in the bowl.

7 Mix all the ingredients together with the wooden spoon until thoroughly combined, with no streaks of flour visible.

8 Spoon the mixture into the prepared tin and spread evenly. ASK AN ADULT TO HELP YOU put the loaf in the preheated oven to bake for 55 minutes, until it's a good golden brown. To test if the loaf is cooked ASK AN ADULT TO HELP YOU carefully remove the loaf from the oven then push a cocktail stick or skewer into the centre of it. If the stick comes out clean the loaf is cooked, if the stick is covered in sticky mixture then bake the loaf for another 5 minutes and test again. ASK AN ADULT TO HELP YOU remove the tin from the oven and put it on a wire rack to cool completely, then remove the loaf from the tin and peel off the paper. Store your banana loaf in an airtight container and eat it within 5 days.

Other ideas
Add 100 g walnut or pecan pieces to the mixture when you mix in the bananas. Or you could try 50 g sultanas or milk chocolate chips.

big bakes

This is a really delicious and chocolatey cake, perfect for birthdays – just decorate it and add candles! It tastes best when it's made the day before the party.

chocolate fudge birthday cake

**Makes 1 large cake that will
   give 8–10 slices**

For the cake:
250 g plain flour
2 teaspoons baking powder
1 teaspoon bicarbonate of soda
a pinch of salt
100 g good plain chocolate
3 tablespoons cocoa powder
100 ml water, very hot but not
   boiling
175 g unsalted butter, softened
250 g caster sugar
3 large free-range eggs
200 ml plain yoghurt (whole
   milk or low-fat NOT fat-free)

For the chocolate icing:
100 ml double cream
50 g good milk chocolate
50 g good plain chocolate

your choice of decorations

*a springform cake tin,
   22.5 cm diameter*
*greaseproof paper or non-stick
   baking parchment*

1 ASK AN ADULT TO HELP YOU preheat the oven to 160°C (325°F) Gas 3.

2 Grease the inside of the cake tin with a little very soft butter on a piece of kitchen paper. Cut a circle from a sheet of greaseproof paper or non-stick baking parchment – put the cake tin on the paper and draw around it. Using scissors, cut inside the line so you have a circle the same size as the tin. Fit this into the bottom of the tin.

3 Set a large sieve over a bowl and tip the flour, baking powder, bicarbonate of soda and salt into the sieve. Carefully sift these ingredients into the bowl. Put the bowl on one side until needed.

4 Break up the plain chocolate and put it into a large heatproof mixing bowl. Mix in the cocoa powder. ASK AN ADULT TO HELP YOU pour on the very hot water. Leave for 1 minute then stir gently with a wooden spoon until the mixture is very smooth and melted. Put on one side.

5 Put the butter and sugar into the bowl of an electric mixer or a mixing bowl. Beat well with the whisk attachment or a wooden spoon.

6 Break the eggs into a small bowl, remove any pieces of shell, then gradually add the eggs to the bowl and beat really well until very smooth.

7 Pour the melted chocolate mixture into the bowl and mix well. Spoon in the yoghurt and tip in the flour mixture and mix well.

8 Spoon the mixture into the prepared tin, then spread the mixture evenly so it is smooth.

9 ASK AN ADULT TO HELP YOU put the cake in the oven to bake for 55 minutes. To test if it is cooked ASK AN ADULT TO HELP YOU remove the cake from the oven and stick a cocktail stick into the middle, then carefully pull it out – the cake is cooked if the stick comes out clean. If the stick is sticky then bake for another 5 minutes and test again. ASK AN ADULT TO HELP YOU remove the cake from the oven and set the tin on a wire rack. Leave to cool for 5 minutes then loosen the cake by running a round-bladed knife inside the tin. Unclip the tin and leave the cake to cool completely. Don't worry if it sinks a bit.

10 To make the icing, put the cream into a saucepan. ASK AN ADULT TO HELP YOU heat it until it is scalding hot, but not quite boiling. Remove the pan from the heat. Break up the two kinds of chocolate and put it in a heatproof bowl. Carefully pour over the hot cream. Leave for about 2 minutes then stir until smooth. Leave to cool, the icing will thicken as it cools.

11 Set the cake upside down on a serving plate. Spread the icing on the top and sides of the cake to cover it completely. Decorate with sprinkles and sweets. Leave in a cool place until it is firm before you cut it. Store your cake in an airtight container and eat it within 5 days.

This is a very rich and moist cake with a hidden layer of golden marzipan. It's perfect for special occasions. Use a bag of mixed dried fruits like sultanas, raisins and currants or try the 'luxury' mix, which also includes chopped apricots and pineapple.

celebration cake

Makes 1 large cake

230 g plain flour
2 teaspoons baking powder
60 g ground almonds
175 g unsalted butter, very soft, plus extra for greasing the tin
175 g light brown muscovado sugar
4 large free-range eggs
2 tablespoons whole milk
350 g dried mixed fruit
230 g ready-made marzipan
2 tablespoons flaked almonds

a round deep cake tin or springform cake tin, 20.5 cm diameter
greaseproof paper or non-stick baking parchment

1 ASK AN ADULT TO HELP YOU preheat the oven to 180°C (350°F) Gas 4.

2 Put a little butter on a piece of kitchen paper and rub it around the inside of the tin. Cut out a circle from a sheet of greaseproof paper or non-stick baking parchment – put the tin on the paper and draw around it. Cut inside the line so you have a circle that fits inside the tin. Fit the circle into the tin so it sticks to the base. Next cut a strip of greaseproof or baking paper the circumference and depth of the tin and fit this inside so it sticks to the sides.

3 Put the flour, baking powder, ground almonds, soft butter and sugar in a large mixing bowl. Break the eggs into the bowl then add the milk. Using a wooden spoon or an electric mixer (on slow speed) beat the mixture for 1 minute, or until it looks very smooth with no streaks.

4 Add the dried fruit to the bowl. Stir well with a wooden spoon until it looks evenly mixed.

5 Spoon half the cake mixture into the tin. Spread it evenly with the back of a spoon.

6 Using your hands, mould and press the marzipan into a round shape 20 cm across. You can also roll out the marzipan with a rolling pin. Place it gently on top of the cake mix in the tin. Spoon the rest of the cake mix on top of the marzipan and spread it evenly. Sprinkle with the flaked almonds.

7 ASK AN ADULT TO HELP YOU put the cake in the preheated oven. Bake for 30 minutes then turn down the oven temperature to 160°C (325°F) Gas 3 and bake for a further 1¼–1½ hours. To test if the cake is cooked, ASK AN ADULT TO HELP YOU remove it from the oven. Push a cocktail stick into the centre of the cake, just down as far as the marzipan layer. If it comes out clean the cake is ready, if it comes out sticky with cake mixture, cook for another 10 minutes.

8 When the cake is cooked, ASK AN ADULT TO HELP YOU remove it from the oven and stand the tin on a wire rack. Leave to cool completely, then turn the cake out of the tin and peel off the lining paper. Store your cake in an airtight container and eat it within a week.

yule log

Makes 1 large cake

For the sponge cake:
115 g caster sugar
4 large free-range eggs, at
    room temperature
½ teaspoon vanilla essence
40 g unsalted butter, plus
    extra for greasing the tin
135 g plain flour
½ teaspoon baking powder

For the filling and icing:
4–5 tablespoons chocolate
    hazelnut spread (Nutella)
100 ml double cream
100 g plain chocolate
icing sugar, to sprinkle
your choice of decorations

a swiss roll tin, 20 x 30 cm
2 sheets non-stick baking
*   parchment*

1 ASK AN ADULT TO HELP YOU preheat the oven to 200°C (400°F) Gas 6. Put a little soft butter on a piece of kitchen paper and rub it around the inside of the tin to lightly grease it. Cut a rectangle of non-stick baking parchment to fit the tin – set the tin on the paper, draw around it then cut just inside the line – and fit it into the tin to completely cover the base.

2 Put the sugar in a mixing bowl or the bowl of an electric mixer. Break the eggs into a small bowl, pick out any pieces of shell, then pour the eggs into the bowl with sugar. Add the vanilla essence. ASK AN ADULT TO HELP YOU melt the butter in a small saucepan over low heat, or in the microwave. Leave to cool until needed.

3 Using an electric whisk or the whisk attachment of the mixer ASK AN ADULT TO HELP YOU whisk the sugar and eggs together for 2 minutes or until very thick and foamy.

4 Set a sieve over the bowl. Tip the flour and baking powder into the sieve and sift it into the bowl. Gently fold into the egg mixture with a large metal spoon. Do this slowly and carefully so the air isn't knocked out of the mixture. Drizzle the melted butter over the top and fold it in quite quickly.

5 Pour the mixture into the prepared tin and spread it evenly using a plastic scraper or spatula. ASK AN ADULT TO HELP YOU put the sponge in the preheated oven to bake for 10 minutes. To test if the sponge is cooked ASK AN ADULT TO HELP YOU pull it out on the oven shelf and press the centre lightly with a finger; if the cake is springy it is cooked, if your finger leaves a dent cook for 2 more minutes then test again.

6 ASK AN ADULT TO HELP YOU remove the sponge from the oven. Leave for 1 minute to cool. Meanwhile cover a wire rack with a dry tea towel, then a sheet of baking parchment. ASK AN ADULT TO HELP YOU carefully tip the sponge out onto the paper. Peel off the lining paper. Gently roll up the sponge with the other sheet of paper still inside. Leave the sponge on the wire rack until it is completely cold.

This is the cake the French make to celebrate Christmas, but its tradition goes back to the time of the pagan Vikings. They had a Yule log ceremony to celebrate the sun at the time of the winter solstice, Yule was Odin, the father of the gods, and a massive log of wood burned in his honour to bring luck. These days a small log is burned at a party on Christmas Eve and is always lit by a piece saved from last year.

The cake is a sponge roll, made by whisking the eggs with an electric mixer or whisk, filled with ready-made chocolate spread, then covered with a rich chocolate cream. You can add decorations like robins, tiny trees, a cake candle, or a small sleigh filled with foil-wrapped sweets or coins for presents.

7 Carefully unroll the sponge and discard the paper – don't worry if the cake has cracked, it will all be covered up, and will still taste good! Spread the chocolate spread over the sponge. Roll up the sponge and put it on a serving plate.

8 Put the cream for the icing in a small saucepan. ASK AN ADULT TO HELP YOU heat the cream until it is steaming hot, but not boiling. Remove the pan from the heat. Break up the plain chocolate and add it to the pan of hot cream. Leave for 2 minutes then stir gently until smooth and melted. Leave until the mixture is thick enough to spread, about 1 hour.

9 Spread the cooled chocolate cream all over the top and sides of your cake. Run the prongs of a fork down the log so it looks like bark on a real tree. Sprinkle with sifted icing sugar 'snow' then add as many decorations as you like.

10 When you are ready to eat your cake remove all of your decorations and ASK AN ADULT TO HELP YOU cut it into round slices. Your yule log is best stored in an airtight container in a cool place and eaten within 3 days.

Just what you need with ice cream and bananas. If you can take the egg whites out of the fridge for an hour before you start it helps a lot. A rotary whisk or electric mixer or whisk and spotlessly clean, and grease-free, bowl are essential to beat the whites to a stiff snow.

chocolate meringues

Makes 12 meringues

75 g good plain chocolate
3 egg whites, from free-range
   eggs
a pinch of cream of tartar
   (optional)
175 g caster sugar

non-stick baking parchment
2 baking trays

1 ASK AN ADULT TO HELP YOU preheat the oven to 120°C (250°F) Gas ½.

2 Cut out 2 rectangles of non-stick baking parchment to fit your baking trays, then put one on each tray.

3 Break up the chocolate and put it in a small heatproof bowl. ASK AN ADULT TO HELP YOU melt the chocolate: half-fill a saucepan with water and carefully put it on the stove and bring it to the boil, turn off the heat then set the bowl over the pan and leave the chocolate to melt gently, stirring every few minutes until smooth. Carefully remove the bowl from the pan and leave to cool slightly while you whisk up the whites.

4 Put the egg whites and cream of tartar, if using, in a large spotlessly clean and grease-free bowl (grease will make it difficult to stiffly whisk the whites). Stand the bowl on a damp tea towel to keep it from wobbling.

5 Using a rotary or electric whisk or mixer start whisking the egg whites. Whisk steadily until the whites turn into a stiff white foam – lift out the whisk and there will be a little peak of white standing on the end, and if you are brave enough to turn the bowl upside down, the whites will remain in the bowl.

6 Tip the sugar on to the whites and whisk it into them to make a stiff and glossy meringue. Stop whisking as soon as all of the sugar has been combined.

7 Drizzle the melted chocolate over the meringue then gently stir through, using a very few strokes so the mixture looks very streaky and marbled.

8 Scoop a heaped tablespoon of the mixture out of the bowl and drop it onto one of the prepared baking trays to make a craggy heap of meringue. Repeat with the rest of the mixture to make 12, spacing them slightly apart on the trays.

9 ASK AN ADULT TO HELP YOU put the meringues in the preheated oven to bake for 2 hours. ASK AN ADULT TO HELP YOU carefully remove the trays from the oven and leave to cool. Peel the meringues off the lining paper and pile them up in a serving bowl. Your meringues can also be stored in an airtight container for up to a week.

Another idea
The meringues can also be made in the same way then shaped into nests, by making a slight hollow in the middle of each one with the back of a spoon. After baking and cooling you can fill them with a scoop of ice cream or fruit.

This is a rich bread dough, made with milk, egg and butter, that is rolled up with sugar, cinnamon and pecans or raisins then cut into spiral buns. Warm from the oven, they smell and taste heavenly. The dough can be made with your hands or using a large electric mixer fitted with a special 'dough hook'.

sticky cinnamon buns

Makes 12 buns

For the dough:
500 g strong white bread flour
1 x 7 g sachet easy-blend
    (fast action) dried yeast
1 teaspoon salt
3 tablespoons caster sugar
1 large free-range egg,
    at room temperature
300 ml milk, lukewarm
40 g unsalted butter, very soft

For the filling:
30 g butter, very soft
1 teaspoon ground cinnamon
4 tablespoons light brown
    muscovado sugar
50 g pecan pieces or raisins

a baking tray, very well
greased

1 Put the flour in a large mixing bowl. Add the yeast, salt and sugar and mix everything with your hand or ASK AN ADULT TO HELP YOU with the mixer dough hook. Make a hollow in the middle of the flour mixture.

2 Mix the egg with the milk and add to the bowl with the very soft butter.

3 Using your hand, slowly stir the flour into the liquid in the hollow, then work the mixture with your hand until all the flour has been mixed in. Flours vary so if there are dry crumbs in the bowl and the dough feels dry add a little more milk, a tablespoonful at a time. If the dough is very sticky add a little more flour. If using the electric mixer use the lowest speed.

4 When the mixture comes together to make a soft dough, gather it into a ball. Sprinkle a little flour over a work surface and tip the dough out of the bowl onto it. Knead the dough with both hands, stretching it out then gathering back into a ball (see pages 58–59) for 5 minutes. The dough can be kneaded using an electric mixer on low speed for 4 minutes.

5 Put the dough back into the mixing bowl and cover the bowl with a snap-on lid or put the bowl into a large, clean plastic bag and tie it closed. Leave the bowl near a warm stove or above a radiator until doubled in size – about 1 hour. It will take longer at normal room temperature or on a cool day.

6 Uncover the bowl and gently punch down the dough with your fist. Sprinkle your work surface lightly with flour then tip the dough onto it.

7 Using your hands, or a rolling pin, press or roll the dough out to a rectangle about 25 x 35 cm. Spread the butter for the filling over the dough. Mix the cinnamon and sugar and sprinkle over the butter. Lastly scatter the nuts or raisins over the dough and lightly press down.

8 Roll up the dough from one of the long sides (like a Swiss roll) to make a long roll, then pinch the 'seam' of the dough to seal it. ASK AN ADULT TO HELP YOU cut it into 12 equal pieces.

9 Put the rolls slightly apart on the prepared baking tray with the cut side facing up so you can see the spiral filling. Cover the tray with a clean, dry tea towel and leave to rise for 20 minutes. Meanwhile ASK AN ADULT TO HELP YOU preheat the oven to 220°C (425°F) Gas 7.

10 Uncover the buns then ASK AN ADULT TO HELP YOU put the tray in the preheated oven to bake for 20 minutes, until golden brown. ASK AN ADULT TO HELP YOU remove the tray from the oven. Use a metal spatula to lift the buns onto a wire rack to cool. Eat warm or at room temperature. Once they are cold you can keep your buns in an airtight container and eat them within 2 days or freeze them for up to 1 month.

This an easy to make all-in-one loaf cake flavoured with fresh orange. Look out for an unwaxed or organic orange, as half of it will be whizzed up in a processor, and the other half used for the topping.

fresh orange cake

Makes 1 large loaf cake

1 unwaxed orange, washed
175 g unsalted butter, very
    soft, plus extra for greasing
    the tin
250 g caster sugar
3 large free-range eggs,
    at room temperature
250 g self-raising flour
1 teaspoon bicarbonate
    of soda
100 ml milk
3 tablespoons plain yoghurt
    (whole milk or low-fat, not
    fat-free)
3 tablespoons caster or
    granulated sugar, for the
    topping

a 900 g loaf tin
greaseproof paper or non-
    stick baking parchment

1 ASK AN ADULT TO HELP YOU preheat the oven to 180°C (350°F) Gas 4. Lightly rub the inside of the loaf tin with a little soft butter on a piece of kitchen paper. Cut a long strip of greaseproof paper or non-stick baking parchment the width of the tin. Press the paper into the tin so it covers the base and the two short sides.

2 Carefully cut the orange in half. Save one half for the topping. Remove the pips from the other half then cut it into 8 pieces. Put the pieces, as they are with the skin still on, in a food processor and ASK AN ADULT TO HELP YOU run the processor until the orange is chopped into very small pieces. ASK AN ADULT TO HELP YOU remove the blade from the processor then transfer the orange mixture to a mixing bowl or the bowl of an electric mixer.

3 Add the very soft butter and sugar to the bowl. Break the eggs into a small bowl, pick out any pieces of shell, then pour the eggs into the mixing bowl.

4 Set a sieve over the bowl. Spoon the flour and bicarbonate of soda into the sieve then sift into the bowl. Add the milk and yoghurt then beat with a wooden spoon or electric mixer (on low speed) for 1 minute until well mixed and there are no streaks of flour visible.

5 Spoon the mixture into the prepared tin and spread the surface to make it smooth.

6 ASK AN ADULT TO HELP YOU put the cake in the preheated oven to bake for about 50 minutes, until a good golden brown. To test if the cake is cooked ASK AN ADULT TO HELP YOU remove it from the oven, then push a cocktail stick into the centre. If the stick comes out clean, then the loaf is ready. If it is sticky with mixture, then cook the loaf for another 5 minutes.

7 While the loaf is cooking, make the topping. Squeeze out the juice from the reserved orange half with a lemon squeezer. Pour the juice into a small bowl, add the sugar and stir for a minute to make a thick, syrupy glaze.

8 When the loaf is cooked, ASK AN ADULT TO HELP YOU remove it from the oven and stand the tin on a wire rack. Prick the top of the loaf all over with a cocktail stick to make lots of small holes in it. Spoon the orange syrup all over the top so it trickles into the holes. Leave until completely cold before carefully removing the cake from the tin. Peel off the lining paper. Cut the cake into thick slices. Store your cake in an airtight container and eat it within 4 days.

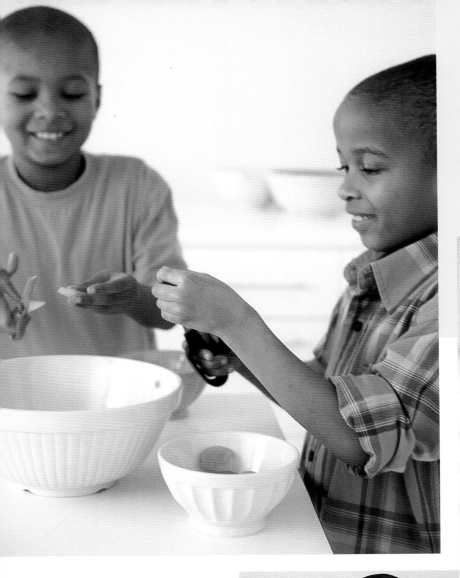

This light golden sponge cake, speckled with pieces of dried fruit, is an ideal bake for several pairs of hands – there's plenty of measuring, cutting up with scissors, and mixing to do.

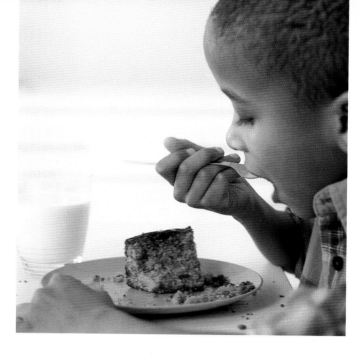

apricot & mango cake

Makes 1 large cake

l unwaxed orange

125 g soft dried apricots

30 g dried mango

175 g plain flour

2 teaspoons baking powder

1 teaspoon ground cinnamon

140 g light brown muscovado
  sugar

3 tablespoons ground
  almonds

3 large free-range eggs

140 g unsalted butter, very
  soft, plus extra for greasing
  the tin

demerara sugar or flaked
  almonds, for sprinkling
  (optional)

*a round deep cake tin or
  springform cake tin, 21 cm
  diameter*
greaseproof paper

1 ASK AN ADULT TO HELP YOU preheat the oven
to 170°C (325°F) Gas 3. Put a little very soft
butter on a piece of kitchen paper and rub it
inside the cake tin so it is lightly coated. Stand
the tin on a sheet of greaseproof paper, draw
around the base of the tin then cut out the circle
just inside the line you have drawn. Fit the circle
into the base of the tin.

2 Rinse and dry the orange. Using a fine grater,
or an orange/lemon zester, grate or zest the
orange peel from the orange into a small bowl,
leaving the white pith on the fruit. Cut the
fruit in half and squeeze out the juice using an
lemon squeezer. Measure 2 tablespoons of the
juice into the bowl with the zest. (You can drink
the rest of the orange juice or use it for a
smoothie.) Using kitchen scissors, carefully cut
the apricots and mango in to small pieces about
the size of your thumbnail. Put them in the bowl
with the juice and zest and give them a stir.
Leave to soak until needed.

3 Set a sieve over a mixing bowl. Tip the flour,
baking powder, cinnamon and sugar into the
sieve then sift into the bowl. Stir in the almonds.

4 Break the eggs into a small bowl. Pick out any
pieces of shell then beat lightly with a fork to
just break up the eggs. Tip into the mixing bowl.
Put the very soft butter into the bowl then mix
everything together with a wooden spoon (or
ASK AN ADULT TO HELP YOU mix with an electric
mixer on medium speed) until very smooth.

5 Add the apricot mixture to the bowl and stir in
gently with a wooden spoon. Spoon the mixture
into the prepared tin and spread evenly. Sprinkle
with demerara sugar or flaked almonds, if using.
ASK AN ADULT TO HELP YOU put the cake in the
preheated oven to bake for 45–50 minutes, until
a good golden brown. To test if the cake is
cooked ASK AN ADULT TO HELP YOU remove the
cake from the oven, push a cocktail stick into the
centre of the cake, if the stick comes out clean
then the cake is cooked. If there is mixture
clinging to it, then bake for 5 minutes more and
test again. ASK AN ADULT TO HELP YOU remove
the cake from the oven and leave to cool for 5
minutes. Remove from the tin and leave to cool
completely on a wire rack. Store your cake in an
airtight container and eat it within 5 days.

The base is like a rich, crisp shortbread, which you can make in a processor or with your hands. Save the leftover egg whites to make meringues (see page 40). For the topping you can use blueberries, apricots, cherries or blackberries.

fresh fruit torte

Makes 1 large torte

For the base:
150 g plain flour
1 teaspoon baking powder
½ teaspoon ground cinnamon
50 g caster sugar
yolks from 2 large free-range
   eggs
50 g unsalted butter, chilled
   and diced
300 g fresh blueberries,
   blackberries or cherries, OR
400 g apricots or plums, rinsed

For the topping:
30 g plain flour
¼ teaspoon ground cinnamon
30 g caster sugar
30 g ground almonds
30 g unsalted butter, chilled
   and diced

*a springform cake tin about
   21.5 cm diameter*
*non-stick baking parchment
   or greaseproof paper*
a baking tray

1 ASK AN ADULT TO HELP YOU preheat the oven to 180°C (350°F) Gas 4.

2 Grease the inside of the cake tin with a small amount of very soft butter on a piece of kitchen paper. Cut a circle from a sheet of non-stick baking parchment or greaseproof paper – put the cake tin on the paper and draw around it. Cut inside the line so you have a circle the size of the tin. Fit it into the bottom of the tin.

3 Put the flour, baking powder, cinnamon and sugar into the bowl of a food processor. ASK AN ADULT TO HELP YOU use the processor to mix the ingredients together. Add the egg yolks and butter to the processor. AGAIN WITH ADULT HELP, work the processor to mix all the ingredients until they look like very large crumbs. You can also make the mixture without a food processor. Put all the ingredients in a mixing bowl and work them together with your fingers.

4 ASK AN ADULT TO HELP YOU remove the blade then tip the crumbs into the cake tin and spread evenly. Press the mixture firmly into the tin with the back of a spoon to make an even layer.

5 Scatter the blueberries or blackberries over the cake mixture. If using cherries, ASK AN ADULT TO HELP YOU remove the stones using a cherry pitter. If using apricots or plums cut in half, then twist to separate the halves of the fruit. Remove the stone then cut each half into 4 slices. Arrange the fruit over the base.

6 Put all the ingredients for the topping into the bowl of the food processor. ASK AN ADULT TO HELP YOU use the processor to mix the ingredients until they look like big breadcrumbs. You can also put all the ingredients into a mixing bowl and squeeze them with your fingers until they come together in pea-sized pieces.

7 Scatter the topping evenly over the fruit. Put the cake tin on a baking tray then ASK AN ADULT TO HELP YOU put the torte in the preheated oven to bake for 35 minutes, until golden brown. ASK AN ADULT TO HELP YOU remove it from the oven. Leave to cool on a wire rack until warm, then gently unclip the tin and remove the torte. It looks good dusted with sifted icing sugar before serving. Eat warm or at room temperature with a dollop of yoghurt.

A deliciously tropical cake made from canned pineapple and desiccated coconut. For the freshest taste use fruit in natural juice rather than sugar syrup, and unsweetened coconut. The easy topping is made from cream cheese mixed with more pineapple.

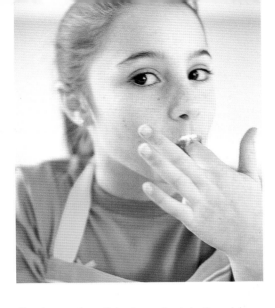

crushed pineapple & coconut cake

Makes 1 large loaf cake

For the cake:
300 g plain flour
2 teaspoons baking powder
a pinch of salt
½ teaspoon ground cinnamon
175 g light brown muscovado sugar
125 g unsalted butter, very soft, plus extra for the tin
2 large free-range eggs
50 g unsweetened desiccated coconut
400 g can pineapple chunks or rings in natural juice

For the topping:
150 g full-fat cream cheese
75 g icing sugar

a 900 g loaf tin
non-stick baking parchment or greaseproof paper

1 ASK AN ADULT TO HELP YOU preheat the oven to 180°C (350°F) Gas 4. Put a little soft butter on a small piece of kitchen paper and rub around the inside of the tin. Cut a strip of baking or greaseproof paper the same width as the tin and long enough to cover the base of the tin and both short ends. Fit the paper into the tin.

2 Set a sieve over a mixing bowl. Tip the flour, baking powder, salt and cinnamon into the sieve and sift into the bowl. Add the sugar and mix well, breaking up any small lumps. Make a well in the centre of the ingredients.

3 Put the soft butter into the well. Break the eggs into a small bowl, pick out any pieces of shell then tip onto the butter. Tip the coconut on top.

4 ASK AN ADULT TO HELP YOU open the can of pineapple. Set a small sieve over a jug or small bowl and drain the pineapple in the sieve. When it has drained, weigh out 150 g of the pineapple and chop it up or cut it into small pieces. Save the rest of the pineapple for the topping. Put the chopped pineapple in the bowl with the eggs, butter and coconut. Measure 125 ml of the pineapple juice and pour it on top of the chopped-up pineapple in the mixing bowl. Save the rest of the juice for the topping.

5 Mix together all the ingredients in the mixing bowl with a wooden spoon, until thoroughly combined. Spoon into the prepared tin and spread evenly. ASK AN ADULT TO HELP YOU put the cake in the preheated oven to bake for about 55 minutes, until golden brown. To test whether the cake is cooked, stick a cocktail stick into the centre of the cake. If it comes out clean then the cake is cooked, if the stick has sticky cake mixture on it then bake for another 5 minutes and test again. ASK AN ADULT TO HELP YOU remove the cake from the oven and leave it to cool on a wire rack. When completely cold run a round-bladed knife around the inside of the tin to loosen the cake then carefully remove it from the tin.

6 To make the topping, put the cream cheese and icing sugar in a small mixing bowl. Add 2 teaspoons of the leftover pineapple juice (you can treat yourself to the rest!) then beat well with a wooden spoon until smooth. Spread the mixture over the top of the cake. Decorate with some of the leftover pineapple pieces (again, you can have the rest). Serve immediately or store your cake in an airtight container in a cool place and eat it within 3 days.

raspberry shortcake

Makes 9 shortcakes

For the base:
200 g plain flour
25 g cornflour
a pinch of salt
75 g caster sugar
150 g unsalted butter, straight
   from the fridge, plus extra
   for the tin

For the filling:
150 g fresh raspberries
125 g good raspberry jam

For the topping:
50 g porridge oats
3 tablespoons light brown
   muscovado sugar

a 18 cm square cake tin

1 ASK AN ADULT TO HELP YOU preheat the oven to 180°C (350°F) Gas 4. Put a little soft butter on a small piece of kitchen paper and rub it around the inside of the tin.

2 Tip the flour, cornflour, salt and sugar into the bowl of a food processor. ASK AN ADULT TO HELP YOU work the processor for a few seconds to mix the ingredients. Cut the butter into small pieces and add to the bowl of the processor. Work the processor until the mixture looks like fine crumbs. Carefully remove the lid and ASK AN ADULT TO HELP YOU remove the blade.

3 Tip the mixture into a bowl. Weigh out 100 g of the mixture and put on one side for the topping. Tip the rest of the mixture into the prepared tin. Give the tin a shake so it is evenly spread then press it down with your hand to make a firm, even layer. If it seems sticky, dip your fingers in a little flour. ASK AN ADULT TO HELP YOU put the shortcake base in the preheated oven to bake for 10 minutes then remove it from the oven. Leave to cool while you make the filling and topping. Leave the oven on.

4 Put the raspberries and conserve or jam into a bowl and mix gently. Put to one side.

5 Put the 100 g shortcake crumbs you saved into another mixing bowl. Add the oats and sugar, mix well then squeeze the mixture together with your hands so it comes together into flakes or large crumbs.

6 Gently spread the raspberry mixture over the baked shortcake. Scatter the oat topping evenly over the raspberries. ASK AN ADULT TO HELP YOU put the tin back into the oven and bake for another 15–20 minutes, until a light golden brown and bubbling around the edges. ASK AN ADULT TO HELP YOU remove the tin from the oven and leave to cool on a wire rack.

7 When completely cold, run a round-bladed knife around the inside of the tin then cut the shortcake into 9 squares. Store your shortcake in an airtight container and eat it within 4 days. It's also really good served with custard as a dessert.

A combination of fine Scottish foods – buttery shortcake covered with fresh raspberries and raspberry jam and then a crunchy oat topping. A bit like a very posh jam tart!

Chocolate and peanut butter are a well-loved combination – you can even buy them in a jar together! These little fairy cakes will please fans of both. But, if you are cooking for a birthday party, remember to label them clearly so anyone with an allergy to peanuts can avoid them.

little peanut butter cakes

Makes 12 small cakes

75 g best-quality smooth
  peanut butter (with no-
  added sugar)
25 g unsalted butter, very soft
100 g light brown muscovado
  sugar
2 large free-range eggs
½ teaspoon vanilla essence
125 g plain flour
1 teaspoon baking powder
4 tablespoons milk
75 g plain chocolate chips,
  plus extra for decorating
icing sugar, for dusting
  (optional)

*a 12-hole muffin tray lined
  with paper muffin cases*
a pastry brush (optional)

1 ASK AN ADULT TO HELP YOU preheat the oven to 180°C (350°F) Gas 4.

2 Put the peanut butter and very soft butter in a large mixing bowl or the bowl of a food mixer. Add the sugar and beat with a wooden spoon or ASK AN ADULT TO HELP YOU use the mixer until well mixed.

3 Break the eggs into a small bowl. Pick out any pieces of shell then add the vanilla essence and break up the eggs with a fork. Add a tablespoon of the eggs to the mixing bowl and beat well. Gradually add all of the egg mixture to the mixing bowl beating well each time.

4 Set a sieve over the mixing bowl. Tip the flour and baking powder into the sieve and sift onto the mixture. Add the milk then gently stir into the other ingredients. When well mixed add the chocolate chips and mix in.

5 Spoon the mixture into the paper muffin cases until they are about one-third full. Sprinkle with chocolate chips.

6 ASK AN ADULT TO HELP YOU put the cakes in the preheated oven to bake for 15–20 minutes, until a light golden colour. ASK AN ADULT TO HELP YOU remove them from the oven and leave to cool on a wire rack.

7 If you want to decorate your cakes ASK AN ADULT TO HELP YOU cut a simple shape, such as a heart or star, out of paper to make a stencil. Hold your stencil over each cake and use a pastry brush dipped in a little milk or water to slightly moisten the area where you want the icing sugar to stick. Lift off the stencil. Put some icing sugar in a small sieve and shake it over the cakes. Next shake each cake and the icing sugar shape will appear. Magic! When cold store your cakes in an airtight container and eat them within 4 days.

breads

making bread

Makes 1 large loaf

**700 g strong white or
wholemeal bread flour
(or 350 g of each)**
1½ teaspoons salt
**1 x 7 g sachet easy-blend
(fast-action) dried yeast**
**425–450 ml lukewarm water
or milk**

a 900 g loaf tin

1 Sift the flour into a large mixing bowl. Add
the salt and dried yeast and mix well with your
hand. You can also make the dough using a large
electric mixer but ASK AN ADULT TO HELP YOU
with this. Put the flour, salt and yeast in the
mixer bowl and use the dough hook attachment
on the lowest speed to mix the ingredients.
Make a well in the middle of the flour.

2 Pour 425 ml lukewarm water into this well.
Using your hands (or the dough hook) slowly stir
the flour into the liquid – the mixture will turn
from a thick batter to a soft dough as more flour
is drawn in. Work the mixture until all the flour
has been mixed in. If there are dry crumbs in the
bowl and the dough feels very dry and hard to
mix, add a little more water, 1 tablespoon at a
time. If the dough is very sticky and sticks to your
fingers or to the sides of the bowl, add a little
more flour, 1 tablespoon at a time.

3 Sprinkle a little flour over the work surface
and tip the dough out of the bowl on to it. Using
both hands, knead the dough by stretching it
away from you as if pulling out a rubber band,
then gather it back into a ball again. Turn the
ball around and stretch the dough out again
then gather it back into a ball. Keep doing this
for about 10 minutes until the dough is soft and
smooth – it's hard work but you can take a little
rest every now and then. You can also knead
the dough in the mixer for 4 minutes on the
lowest speed.

4 Put the kneaded dough back into the mixing
bowl – it now has to be left to rise. The yeast
dough needs to be kept warm and moist for
the yeast to thrive and do its work, so cover the
bowl with a snap-on lid or put the bowl into
a large, clean plastic bag or carrier bag and tie
it closed.

How to bake a good home-made loaf

Nothing tastes or smells as wonderful as your first loaf of home-made bread. It's not difficult, it's cheap (you only need four things – proper bread flour, salt, yeast and lukewarm water) and not much can go wrong. You can kill the yeast with too much heat – if the mixing liquid is too hot for your little finger it's too hot for the yeast (it's a living fungus, believe it or not, just 'resting' in its little sachet). Here's the basic recipe, you can use it to make a loaf or rolls, or add fruit and nuts or seeds.

5 If you leave the bowl near a warm oven or above a radiator it will take about an hour to double in size. At normal room temperature it will take 1½–2 hours, depending on the time of year. Left in a cool room allow 2–6 hours, or you can leave it overnight in the fridge.

6 While the dough is rising, put some soft butter on a piece of kitchen paper and rub it inside the loaf tin to grease it.

7 When the dough has doubled in size, uncover the bowl and gently punch down the dough with your fist. Sprinkle your work surface lightly with flour then tip the dough out onto it. Shape the dough into a brick to fit your tin. Lift the dough into the tin and gently press it down.

8 Put the tin in a plastic bag again and let the dough rise in a warm place until doubled in size. This should take about 1 hour.

9 ASK AN ADULT TO HELP YOU preheat the oven to 220°C (425°F) Gas 7. Uncover the dough and ASK AN ADULT TO HELP YOU carefully put the tin in the oven. Bake it for 35 minutes until the loaf is a good golden brown. WITH ADULT HELP, carefully remove the tin from the oven and tip the bread out of the tin onto a wire rack to cool.

10 To make sure the bread is cooked right through, carefully (the bread is very hot) tap the underside of the loaf with the back of your hand – it should sound hollow like a drum. If you hear a dull thud then put the loaf (without the tin) back in the oven for another 5 minutes then test again in the same way.

11 Leave the bread to cool completely on the wire rack before cutting. Eat your loaf within 5 days or freeze it for up to a month.

Other ideas

The same dough can be shaped into rolls instead of a loaf shape: divide the dough into 15 even pieces. Dip your hands in a little flour then roll the dough into balls, sausage shapes, twists, or make them into animal shapes with raisins for eyes, or flatten the balls to make hamburger buns or baps. Let rise, spaced well apart on 2 well-greased baking trays, then bake in the preheated oven for 15–20 minutes, depending on the thickness of the rolls.

The same dough can be made into a sunflower loaf: when you make up the dough add 3 tablespoons sunflower seeds (or a ready-made seed mixture) to the flour with the salt and yeast. Mix well then add 1 tablespoon honey to the lukewarm water and use to make the dough. While the dough is rising the first time, rub a little soft butter inside the tin then scatter a tablespoon of seeds inside the tin. When you have put the shaped dough into the tin lightly brush the top with a little milk or water then scatter another tablespoon of seeds over the top. Leave to rise again then bake as above.

You can also use the dough to make a fruit loaf: add 75 g caster sugar to the flour with the salt and yeast (at Easter time you can make a hot cross bun dough by also adding 1½ teaspoons

ground mixed spice) and 125 g mixed dried fruit. Mix well then mix 1 egg with 375 ml lukewarm milk and add to the bowl instead of the water to make the dough. After kneading, leave the dough to rise as above, then shape into a loaf or a large plait or into 15 buns. Leave to double in size then bake as above.

To make your bread shiny: just before baking the bread, dip a pastry brush into a little beaten egg or milk and carefully brush over the top of the dough, but don't let it drip onto the tin or the baking tray (otherwise the dough might become 'glued on' during baking).

My son Dan wanted to make a stripy loaf of bread for a school project, so he tried layering the dough with different ingredients, and this is the one we all liked the best. It's very good toasted.

red bread

Makes 1 large loaf

400 g strong white bread flour
100 g strong wholemeal bread
flour or spelt flour
1 teaspoon salt
1 x 7 g sachet easy-blend
(fast-action) dried yeast
325 ml lukewarm water
200 g Red Leicester cheese or
Mrs Appleby's Cheshire
cheese, grated

a non-stick baking tray,
greased

1 Put both flours, salt and dried yeast in a mixing bowl and mix everything well with your hand or ASK AN ADULT TO HELP YOU put it in the bowl of an electric mixer and use the dough hook attachment.

2 Pour the lukewarm water into the bowl and mix with the flour using your hand, or on low speed if using a mixer, to make a soft dough. If there are dry crumbs at the bottom of the bowl that won't mix in, add more water 1 tablespoon at a time. If the dough is sticky and clings to your hands or the bowl, work in a little more flour.

3 Sprinkle a little flour over the work surface and tip the dough out onto it. Using both hands, knead the dough by stretching it away from you then gathering it back into a ball again. Keep doing this for about 10 minutes. You can also knead the dough in the mixer – it will take 4 minutes at very low speed.

4 Put the kneaded dough back into the mixing bowl – it now has to be left to rise. Cover the bowl with a snap-on lid or put the bowl into a large clean plastic bag and tie it closed. Leave the bowl near a warm oven or radiator for about an hour or until the dough has doubled in size.

5 Uncover the risen dough and gently punch down the dough with your fist. Sprinkle the work surface with flour then tip the dough out onto it. Using a rolling pin, roll out the dough away from you to a long thin rectangle about 18 x 40 cm. Sprinkle the grated cheese over the bottom two thirds of the dough, leaving the top third of the dough uncovered. Gently press the cheese onto the dough to make an even layer.

6 You now have to fold the dough into three, like an envelope. Fold the top uncovered portion of dough down to cover the centre portion of dough. Now fold up the bottom portion of dough to cover the rest of the dough – to make three layers of dough. Have a rest for 5 minutes.

7 Roll out the dough to a rectangle again and repeat step 6 (without adding more cheese) to make 9 layers of dough. Do this step once more and you should now have 27 layers of dough!

8 Use your hands to roll the dough into a sausage about 60 cm long, then tie a knot or make the sausage a bit longer and cut it into 3 then plait together. Set on the baking tray.

9 Cover the dough by slipping the tray into a plastic bag or covering it with a clean, slightly damp tea towel. Leave to rise in a warm place for about 50 minutes, until almost doubled in size. ASK AN ADULT TO HELP YOU preheat the oven to 220°C (425°F) Gas 7.

10 Uncover the bread and ASK AN ADULT TO HELP YOU put it in the preheated oven to bake for about 30 minutes, until a golden brown. ASK AN ADULT TO HELP YOU carefully remove the baking tray from the oven and transfer the bread to a wire rack to cool. When cold, store your loaf in an airtight container and eat it within 3 days.

A fun way to make a loaf – the dough is divided into small pieces
then dipped in melted butter, rolled in cinnamon sugar and nuts
then piled into a loaf tin. A delicious treat!

monkey bread

Makes 1 large loaf

**500 g unbleached strong
white bread flour**

1 teaspoon salt

**1 x 7 g sachet easy-blend
(fast-action) dried yeast**

3 tablespoons caster sugar

50 g unsalted butter, melted

**1 large free-range egg, at
room temperature**

200 ml lukewarm milk

½ teaspoon vanilla essence

100 g pecan pieces

**4 tablespoons dark brown
muscovado sugar**

2 teaspoons ground cinnamon

60 g unsalted butter, melted

a 900 g loaf tin, well-greased

1 Put the flour, salt, dried yeast and caster sugar in a large mixing bowl. Mix everything together with your hand. Make a well in the middle of the mixture.

2 Pour the melted butter into the well. Break the egg into a small bowl and pick out any pieces of shell. Beat with a fork just to break up the egg. Pour into the well with the lukewarm milk and vanilla essence. Use your hand to mix the flour into the liquids in the centre – the mixture will turn from a thick batter to a dough as more flour is drawn in. Work the mixture with your hand until you have a soft, smooth dough. If there are dry crumbs and the dough feels dry and hard to work, gradually add a little more milk 1 tablespoon at a time.

3 Scatter a little flour over the clean work surface. Tip the dough out onto it and knead the dough by stretching it away from you then gathering it back into a ball. Keep doing this for about 5 minutes until the dough feels very springy and smooth. You can also make and knead the dough in a large electric mixer with a dough hook attachment – it will take 4 minutes to knead on very low speed. ASK AN ADULT TO HELP YOU with this.

4 Put the kneaded dough back into the mixing bowl – it now has to be left to rise. Cover the bowl with a snap-on lid or put the bowl into a large clean plastic bag and tie it closed.

5 Leave in a warm place, near the oven or radiator, until doubled in size – for about 1 hour. It will take longer in a cooler place. Uncover the bowl and gently punch down the dough with your fist to knock out the air. Remove from bowl.

6 Scatter a little flour over the work surface then divide the dough into 32 even pieces – you can do this by pulling off small lumps or by shaping the dough into a log and cutting it in half then keep dividing it until you have 32 pieces.

7 Put the pecan pieces, brown sugar and cinnamon in a small bowl and mix well. Dip a piece of dough into the melted butter then into the nut mixture and put in the prepared tin. Keep doing this until all the pieces of dough have been dipped and put in the tin. They do not have to be arranged too neatly, they can look quite higgledy-piggledy and there can be gaps in between them. Cover the loaf tin with a clean, dry tea towel and leave to rise in a warm place for 40 minutes. While the dough is rising, ASK AN ADULT TO HELP YOU preheat the oven to 200°C (400°F) Gas 6.

8 Uncover the tin and again, WITH ADULT HELP, put it into the preheated oven to bake for 30 minutes, until golden brown. ASK AN ADULT TO HELP YOU remove it from the oven and leave for 5 minutes before turning out onto a wire rack. Serve warm. Store your bread in an airtight container and eat it within 4 days.

tomato pesto rolls

Makes 10 small rolls

500 g self-raising flour
½ teaspoon salt
250 g natural cottage cheese
a small bunch of fresh basil,
save 10 leaves for
decoration
1 large free-range egg
about 150 ml milk
5 cherry tomatoes, halved
2 tablespoons pesto (basil
pesto or sun-dried tomato
pesto) or olive oil

a non-stick baking tray

1 ASK AN ADULT TO HELP YOU preheat the oven to 190°C (375°F) Gas 5. Sprinkle a little flour over the baking tray and put it to one side.

2 Put the flour, salt, cottage cheese and basil into the bowl of a food processor. WITH ADULT HELP, run the machine until the ingredients are just mixed, and look like crumbs.

3 Break the egg into a jug, pick out any pieces of shell then add 150 ml milk and beat with a fork, just to combine the egg and milk.

4 WITH ADULT HELP, run the machine and pour in the egg/milk mix through the feed tube. Stop the processor when the ingredients have come together to make a ball of soft dough. If there are dry crumbs and the dough feels hard and dry add a little more milk.

5 Sprinkle a little flour over the work surface. ASK AN ADULT to remove the processor blade then turn out the dough onto the work surface. Flour your hands then gently work and knead the dough twice so it looks smoother.

6 Divide the dough into 10 equal pieces and shape each into a ball. Arrange the balls slightly apart on the prepared baking tray. Make a deep hole in the centre of each with your finger. Push a basil leaf into each hole then a tomato half – cut-side up. Make sure the tomato is deep in the hole in the dough (or it will pop right out during baking!). Brush the top of each roll with the pesto or olive oil.

7 ASK AN ADULT TO HELP YOU put the rolls in the preheated oven to bake for about 20 minutes, until they are golden brown. ASK AN ADULT TO

Here the dough is mixed in a food processor for speed, though you can also make it with your hands. It is made with cottage cheese, which is packed with calcium and good for your bones and teeth. I've given recipes for two flavours – one with tomatoes and pesto and a sweet version, with honey and fresh or dried fruits.

HELP YOU take the rolls out of the oven and carefully put them on a wire rack. Leave to cool until just warm. Eat immediately or the same day. They can also be split in half and toasted the next day, or frozen for up to 1 month.

For make sweet fruit rolls: Follow the recipe opposite but leave out the basil, tomatoes and pesto or oil. Instead, add 1 tablespoon of runny honey to the processor with the cottage cheese

mixture. Make the dough as for the method opposite, then turn it out onto the work surface. Scatter 3 tablespoons of fresh blueberries, 2 tablespoons of dried cherries or chopped, ready-to-eat dried apricots over the dough and knead them into it. Shape into 10 rolls and arrange on the baking tray then ASK AN ADULT TO HELP YOU put them in the preheated oven to bake for about 20 minutes.

The traditional bread of rural Ireland was made at home, and baked in a heavy iron pot set over a peat fire. The breads were quickly made – no kneading or rising – and the light texture comes from mixing the flour with buttermilk which is acidic and reacts with the alkaline bicarbonate of soda to make bubbles of carbon dioxide. Soda bread is best eaten on the day it is baked.

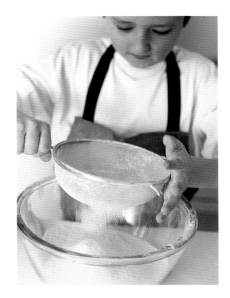

irish soda bread

Makes 1 medium loaf

White soda bread
450 g good-quality plain white flour
1 teaspoon salt
1¼ teaspoons bicarbonate of soda
about 350 ml buttermilk (or 175 ml each natural yoghurt and milk)

a non-stick baking tray

1 ASK AN ADULT TO HELP YOU preheat the oven to 220°C (425°F) Gas 7. Scatter a little flour over the baking tray and put to one side.

2 Set a large sieve over a large mixing bowl. Tip the flour into the sieve, add the salt and bicarbonate of soda and sift into the bowl. Make a well in the centre.

3 Pour the buttermilk into the well. Mix everything together with a round-bladed table knife, or with your hands, to make a soft and slightly sticky dough. Don't worry if it looks a bit rough.

4 Scatter a little flour onto your work surface, then turn out the dough onto it. Dust your hands with flour then gently shape the dough into a ball.

5 Set the ball of dough on the prepared baking tray and flatten it slightly so it is 3–4 cm high. Using the same table knife, score the dough into 4 quarters.

6 ASK AN ADULT TO HELP YOU put the loaf in the preheated oven to bake for about 35 minutes, until a good golden brown. ASK AN ADULT TO

HELP YOU remove it from the oven and tip it upside down onto a wire rack, then tap the underside with your knuckles. The loaf is cooked if it sounds hollow. If it sounds like a dull 'thud' bake it for 5 minutes more. Leave to cool on the wire rack until cool enough to slice.

For speckled white soda bread: Add 100 g chopped plain chocolate or chocolate chips, and 1 tablespoon caster sugar to the bowl with the sifted flour. Mix then finish the recipe as above.

For brown soda bread: The coarse brown wheaten flour traditionally used is hard to find outside Ireland, but a mix of plain wholemeal flour (stoneground if possible), white flour and wheatbran and wheatgerm (from wholefood shops) works well. To make a brown loaf, replace the white flour in the recipe for white soda bread (see left) with 200 g good-quality plain white flour, 200 g plain wholemeal flour and 50 g wheatbran and wheatgerm mix or 25 g of each. Follow the recipe by mixing all the dry ingredients together (but don't sift them into the bowl), then mix to a soft dough with the buttermilk. Shape and bake the loaf as for the white soda bread loaf.

Unlike most bread doughs that need a lot of kneading for a good texture, this one is dead simple. The good, brioche-like taste, texture and smell comes from the Swiss Emmental cheese plus eggs, yet the dough is mixed in the bowl with your hands or with a large electric mixer and left to rise just once, in the tin, before baking. Eat it thickly sliced with tomato soup, or salads, or use for sandwiches, toast or grilled cheese sandwiches.

no-knead cheese bread

Makes 1 large loaf

500 g strong white bread flour
1½ teaspoons salt
¼ teaspoon freshly ground black pepper
¼ teaspoon mustard powder (optional)
a good pinch of cayenne pepper (or a little more if you like it spicy)
1 x 7 g sachet easy-blend (fast-action) dried yeast
100 g Emmental cheese, grated
4 large free-range eggs, at room temperature
250 ml milk, lukewarm (read method, right)

a 900 g loaf tin

1 Put a little soft butter on a piece of kitchen paper and rub it around the inside of the tin.

2 Put the flour in a large mixing bowl, or the bowl of a large electric mixer. Add the salt, black pepper, mustard powder, cayenne pepper and dried yeast. Mix all these ingredients well with your hand, or WITH ADULT HELP, the dough hook attachment of the mixer.

3 Mix in the grated cheese then make a well in the centre of the ingredients. Break the eggs into a small bowl, pick out any pieces of shell then beat with a fork just to break up the eggs. Pour into the well in the flour mixture.

4 To encourage the yeast to grow and produce the carbon dioxide that makes your dough rise it is ideal to use lukewarm milk, about the same temperature as your body. If the milk is too hot the yeast will be killed, if it is too cool then they will take a long time to become active. Gently heat the milk in a small pan over low heat, or in the microwave. Dip your finger into the milk – it should feel just warm and comfortable, not too hot or too chilly. Pour the milk onto the eggs.

5 Using your hand, or WITH ADULT HELP, the dough hook attachment (use the lowest speed on the mixer) work the flour into the eggs and milk to make a soft and sticky dough. Mix the dough in the bowl for 2 minutes, until the dough leaves the sides of the bowl clean.

6 Scrape the dough out of the bowl into the prepared tin and press it evenly into the tin. If it feels very sticky dip your fingers into a little flour.

7 Put the bowl into a large clean plastic bag or carrier bag and tie it closed, making sure the bag is slightly inflated so the plastic doesn't stick to the dough. Leave in a warm spot until the dough doubles in size and just about reaches the top of the tin – about 1½–2 hours, depending on the room temperature. Towards the end of this time ASK AN ADULT TO HELP YOU preheat the oven to 190°C (375°F) Gas 5.

8 Uncover the dough and ASK AN ADULT TO HELP YOU put the loaf in the preheated oven to bake for 45–50 minutes, until golden brown. To test if the loaf is cooked, ASK AN ADULT TO HELP YOU remove it from the oven and tip it out of the tin upside down onto a wire rack. Tap the base of the loaf with your knuckles – if it sounds hollow like a drum, the loaf is cooked, but if it sounds like a dull 'thud' then you need to cook the loaf for another 5 minutes. When ready, leave to cool on the wire rack. Eat your loaf within 4 days or freeze it for up to 1 month.

This is an Italian bread with a tasty filling, to eat with salad or soup. I've given you some ideas for the filling, but it's fun to experiment and find out what you like the best.

stuffed focaccia

Makes 1 large loaf

For the dough:
700 g strong white bread flour
1 x 7 g sachet easy-blend (fast-action) dried yeast
1½ teaspoons salt
½ teaspoon dried mixed herbs or *Herbes de Provence*
425 ml lukewarm water
2 tablespoons olive oil

For the filling:
100 g thinly sliced Italian pepperoni or Spanish chorizo, or prosciutto, or ham, or smoked turkey
1 jar (250 g–300 g), roasted or grilled sweet peppers or sun-dried tomatoes in oil
200 g feta cheese or mild goats' cheese
2–3 tablespoons olive oil

a small non-stick roasting tin, about 22 x 30 cm

1 Tip the flour into a large mixing bowl or ASK AN ADULT TO HELP YOU put it in the bowl of an electric mixer. Add the dried yeast powder, salt and herbs and mix well with your hand or ASK AN ADULT TO HELP YOU with the dough hook attachment of the electric mixer.

2 Make a well in the middle and pour in the lukewarm water and the olive oil. Gradually work the flour into the liquid with your hands or the dough hook set on low speed.

3 When the mixture comes together to make a ball of soft dough that leaves the sides of the bowl clean, scatter a little flour on your work surface and tip the dough out onto it. Now you have to knead the dough for 10 minutes: first use the heel of your hand to stretch the dough away from you as if pulling out a rubber band, then gather it back into a ball. Turn the dough around and repeat this whole stretching out and gathering back process until the dough feels very smooth and elastic. You can also knead the dough in the mixer for 5 minutes on low speed. Put the ball of dough back into the bowl and leave it to rest while you make the filling.

4 Separate the slices of pepperoni, chorizo or ham, and remove any outer skin from the pepperoni. Drain the peppers (saving the oil), then carefully cut into thick slices. Drain the cheese, if necessary, then cut into small cubes. Brush the inside of the tin with a little olive oil.

5 Divide the dough in half. Pat and stretch one piece of the dough to a rectangle the same size as the prepared tin. Fit the dough into the tin, pressing it into the corners.

6 Cover the dough with the slices of pepperoni, chorizo or ham, then scatter the peppers over, then finally top with the cubes of cheese.

7 Press out the remaining piece of dough to a rectangle the size of the tin then gently lay it over the filling. Press it down very gently then seal the edges of the two pieces of dough by pinching them with your fingers. Carefully prick the top of the loaf all over with a cocktail stick or skewer to get rid of any air bubbles trapped between the layers. Slide the tin into a large plastic bag or clean carrier bag, inflate the bag slightly so the plastic doesn't stick to the dough then tie it closed. Leave for 1 hour in a warm spot so the dough about doubles in size.

8 While the dough is rising, ASK AN ADULT TO HELP YOU preheat the oven to 220°C (425°F) Gas 7.

9 Uncover the risen dough and brush with the saved pepper oil or the rest of the olive oil. ASK AN ADULT TO HELP YOU put the focaccia in the preheated oven to bake for 25 minutes, until golden brown. ASK AN ADULT TO HELP YOU remove the tin from the oven and carefully turn it out onto a wire rack to cool. Eat your focaccia warm or at room temperature on the same day.

savoury things

French toast is usually made from bread soaked in a sweet egg and milk mix then fried in butter, but this savoury version is more nutritious and makes a good snack.

canadian french toast

Serves 4–6

½ **baguette or French stick (can be a bit stale)**
4 **large free-range eggs**
300 **ml whole milk or Jersey milk**
freshly ground black pepper
180 **g thin rashers rindless smoked streaky bacon**
100 **g Gruyère cheese, or Cheddar cheese, grated**

a large shallow ovenproof baking dish, about 2 litres capacity

1 ASK AN ADULT TO HELP YOU preheat the oven to 200°C (400°F) Gas 6. Lightly rub the inside of the baking dish with a little soft butter on a piece of kitchen paper. Put it to one side.

2 Carefully cut the bread into slices about 2 cm thick, then fit the slices into the prepared dish like a jigsaw puzzle, slightly squashing them so that they fit together tightly.

3 Break the eggs into a mixing bowl. Pick out any pieces of shell. Pour in the milk, then add several grinds of black pepper, at least 3 but up to 6 if you like your food a bit hot. With a rotary whisk or wire whisk, beat the mixture until it looks very frothy.

4 Pour the egg mixture evenly over the bread. Snip the rashers of bacon in half with kitchen scissors, then arrange the bacon over the top of the bread. Scatter the grated cheese evenly over the top.

5 ASK AN ADULT TO HELP YOU put the Canadian French toast in the preheated oven to bake for about 20 minutes, until golden. ASK AN ADULT TO HELP YOU carefully remove the dish from the oven and eat at once.

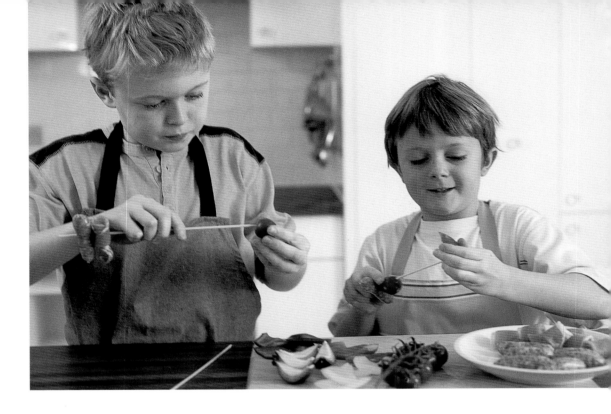

breakfast kebabs

Makes 4 kebabs

8 cherry tomatoes or baby plum tomatoes
½ red pepper
½ green pepper
½ yellow pepper
8 small 'cocktail' sausages
4 rashers back bacon
1 small red onion
4 soft wholemeal rolls or pita breads

4 wooden skewers
a large roasting tin, greased

1 ASK AN ADULT TO HELP YOU preheat the oven to 220°C (425°F) Gas 7. Soak the wooden skewers in warm water for 10 minutes. Be careful with these as they have sharp ends.

2 Meanwhile prepare the vegetables: rinse the tomatoes and peppers under the cold tap, and drain well in a colander. Leave the tomatoes whole. Pull out any core and seeds from the peppers. ASK AN ADULT TO HELP YOU cut each piece of pepper into quarters using a small sharp knife.

3 Using kitchen scissors snip the links between the sausages. Cut each rasher of bacon in half, then roll up. Peel the papery skin off the onion then WITH ADULT HELP, cut it into quarters.

4 Thread the tomatoes, peppers, sausages, bacon and onion onto the wooden skewers, making sure there is a small gap between each piece on the skewer. You can put them in any order you like, but make sure each skewer has an equal amount of each ingredient.

5 Arrange the skewers in the prepared roasting tin, slightly apart. ASK AN ADULT TO HELP YOU put the kebabs in the preheated oven to bake for 15–20 minutes, until golden. Meanwhile ASK AN ADULT TO HELP YOU warm the bread rolls or pita breads, either in the toaster or in a second oven on low temperature. ASK AN ADULT TO HELP YOU remove the kebabs from the roasting tin (you might find kitchen tongs helpful) and put a kebab on each serving plate. Serve immediately with the warmed bread.

My son Dan came up with this recipe for a school project on healthy breakfasts and brunches. The onion can be replaced with a large, flat, field mushroom (quartered). You could add scrambled eggs, and a glass of orange juice.

These deliciously crumbly and flaky pastry straws are given extra flavour with cheese, mustard and a red spice called paprika. They make a tasty and filling snack any time of day. You could also make the fruity salad recipe I've given here and serve it with the straws (still warm from the oven) as a starter before you eat your dinner.

giant cheese straws

Makes 18 cheese straws

For the straws:
375 g pack ready-rolled puff pastry
2 tablespoons grainy mustard (or mild mustard)
1 teaspoon mild paprika
100 g grated Grana Padano cheese (or Parmesan)

For the salad:
6 slices seedless watermelon (about 1 kg or half a small watermelon)
200 g feta cheese
85 g bag ready-washed watercress (or salad leaves)
2 tablespoons pitted black and green olives

2 non-stick baking trays, well greased

1 Let the pastry defrost if it is frozen. Unwrap and gently unroll and flatten the sheet of pastry It should measure about 23 x 37 cm. If your pastry is a different size don't worry, as long as you can cut it into strips about 2 cm wide and about 20 cm long it will work.

2 Mix the mustard with the paprika and spread evenly over the pastry. Sprinkle the cheese in an even layer over the top then gently press the cheese onto the pastry.

3 Cut the pastry into 18 even strips each 23 cm long. Take one strip and hold an end in each hand then twist the straw towards the middle. Put down onto the work surface and gently roll it as if making a sausage from play dough, so the twist picks up any cheese that has dropped off, and is tightly twisted.

4 Put the twist on the prepared baking tray, and make the rest in the same way.

5 Chill the straws in the fridge for 15 minutes. Meanwhile, ASK AN ADULT TO HELP YOU preheat the oven to 200°C (400°F) Gas 6.

6 ASK AN ADULT TO HELP YOU put the baking trays in the preheated oven to bake for about 15 minutes, until golden brown and crispy.

7 ASK AN ADULT TO HELP YOU remove the trays from the oven. Leave the straws to cool on the trays for 5 minutes then carefully lift the straws onto a wire rack using a metal spatula, and leave to cool completely. Eat as soon as possible or store in an airtight container for up to 2 days.

8 To make the salad, ASK AN ADULT TO HELP YOU cut away the rind from the watermelon slices. Carefully cut the watermelon into cubes about 3 cm in size. Drain the feta cheese if necessary then cut it into cubes the same size as the watermelon pieces.

9 Put the watercress into a salad bowl. Scatter the watermelon and feta on top then finally the olives. Eat the salad as soon as possible with the cheese straws.

crostini

Makes 4 crostini

4 large thick slices bread
12 cherry tomatoes or baby
**   plum tomatoes**
4 fresh basil leaves
8 pitted black olives
3 tablespoons olive oil
freshly ground black pepper
1 large garlic clove

a large baking tray

1 ASK AN ADULT TO HELP YOU preheat the oven to its hottest setting, usually 240°C (475°F) Gas 9. Arrange the slices of bread on the baking tray. ASK AN ADULT TO HELP YOU put the bread in the preheated oven to bake for 5 minutes, until golden brown. ASK AN ADULT TO HELP YOU remove the tray from the oven and put the bread slices onto serving plates.

2 While the bread is baking, rinse the tomatoes under cold running water and drain well. ASK AN ADULT TO HELP YOU cut the tomatoes into quarters. Put into a small mixing bowl. Tear up the basil leaves into little pieces and add to the tomatoes. Quarter the olives and add to the bowl with the olive oil and black pepper. Stir gently to mix.

3 Slice the garlic clove in half and rub the cut sides over the hot bread slices. Spoon the tomato mixture over the bread and eat straight away.

Some more ideas

Drain a small (200 g) can tuna and flake the fish with a fork. Arrange on top of the tomato mixture.

Cut a 150 g ball mozzarella cheese into small cubes. Arrange on top of the tomato mixture.

Top the tomato mixture with rocket leaves and 100 g thinly sliced ham.

Drain a small (200 g) can tuna and WITH ADULT HELP, put it in the bowl of a food processor with 2 anchovy fillets, the juice of a lemon, 2 tablespoons mayonnaise and several grinds of black pepper. WITH ADULT HELP process to make a thick paste and spread over the bread.

This warm snack is very quick to make. Slices of bread are baked in the oven to make them crispy, then rubbed with garlic and topped with a tomato mixture. You will need good bread – try a baguette that is at least a day old, or an Italian country-style bread like pane pugliese or pane rustica.

Good for parties and picnics, as well as lunch boxes, these savoury muffins are filled with molten cheese and spicy Spanish sausage.

chorizo & cheese muffins

Makes 12 muffins

500 g plain flour
2 teaspoons baking powder
a pinch of salt
freshly ground black pepper
230 g Emmental, Gruyère or Appenzeller cheese
100 g thickly sliced chorizo sausage (or ham, or canned or frozen sweetcorn kernels)
2 large free-range eggs
100 g unsalted butter
350 ml whole milk

12-hole muffin tray lined with paper muffin cases

1 ASK AN ADULT TO HELP YOU preheat the oven to 200°C (400°F) Gas 6.

2 Set a large sieve over a mixing bowl. Tip the flour into the sieve, then add the baking powder, salt and a few grinds of pepper and sift these ingredients into the bowl.

3 ASK AN ADULT TO HELP YOU carefully cut the cheese into small cubes. Add these to the bowl. Using kitchen scissors, cut up the chorizo into pieces about the same size as the cheese. Add to the bowl and mix well. Make a well in the centre of the mixture.

4 Break the eggs into a bowl. Pick out any pieces of shell then beat the eggs with a fork until just broken up. Pour into the well in the mixture in the mixing bowl.

5 Put the butter in a small saucepan and ASK AN ADULT TO HELP YOU melt the butter over very low heat. The butter can also be melted in a microwave. Pour into the well in the mixture in the mixing bowl, along with the milk.

6 Mix all the ingredients together with a wooden spoon to make a rough-looking mixture. Spoon this mixture into the prepared muffin cases, making sure there is the same amount in each one.

7 ASK AN ADULT TO HELP YOU put the muffins in the preheated oven to bake for 30 minutes, until golden brown. ASK AN ADULT TO HELP YOU remove the tray from the oven, leave to cool for a couple of minutes then transfer the muffins to a wire rack and leave to cool completely. Eat warm or at room temperature the same or the next day and store in an airtight container.

A frittata is an Italian omelette, and this one is full of vegetables plus cheese. Instead of making the frittata in a large frying pan these are baked in a muffin tray to make 12 small ones – perfect if you are having friends round (allow one per person for a first course, or two or even three for a main dish). Good with salad leaves and potato salad.

mini vegetable frittatas

Makes 12 mini frittatas

4 spring onions
3 medium courgettes
1 medium red pepper
100 g soft sun-dried tomatoes
125 g Fontina cheese (or
 Gruyère or Swiss cheese)
8 large free-range eggs
125 ml single cream
freshly ground black pepper
2 tablespoons olive oil
a good pinch of dried oregano

12-hole muffin tray, well
 greased or 12 flexible
 muffin moulds
a baking tray

1 ASK AN ADULT TO HELP YOU preheat the oven to 180°C (350°F) Gas 4. WITH ADULT HELP and using a small sharp knife, carefully trim the hairy root ends off the spring onions, and the dark green leafy tops. Rinse the onions well under the cold tap, and drain thoroughly. Slice into thin rounds then put to one side.

2 Rinse the courgettes, then trim off the ends. Slice each courgette in half lengthways then cut each half in half lengthways so you have 4 long strips from each courgette. Cut the strips across to make 1 cm pieces. Put with the spring onions.

3 Rinse the red pepper. Cut off the stalk end, then cut the pepper in half and pull out the core with its seeds. Slice the red flesh of the pepper into strips about 1 cm wide, then cut each strip across to make 1 cm pieces. Add to the onions.

4 Cut the sun-dried tomatoes into 1 cm pieces but keep separate from the onion mixture.

5 Cut the cheese into 1 cm cubes and add to the tomatoes.

6 Break the eggs into a bowl. Pick out any pieces of shell. Pour the cream into the bowl, add several grinds of black pepper then, using a table fork, gently beat the eggs and cream together until thoroughly mixed.

7 Spoon the olive oil into a medium frying pan. ASK AN ADULT TO HELP YOU gently heat it on the stove. Put the spring onions, courgettes, red pepper and a good pinch of oregano into the pan and stir well with a wooden spoon. Turn up the heat to medium and cook for 5 minutes, stirring carefully every minute, until the vegetables are a light golden brown. ASK AN ADULT TO HELP YOU remove the pan from the heat and put it onto a heatproof surface.

8 Leave to cool for 5 minutes then stir in the tomatoes and cheese.

9 Set the muffin tray on a baking tray. Spoon the vegetable and cheese mixture into the holes, filling each one with an equal amount. Using a small ladle or spoon, pour the egg mix over the vegetable mixture (you may find it easier to transfer the egg mix to a large jug then pour the mix onto the vegetables).

10 ASK AN ADULT TO HELP YOU put the frittatas in the preheated oven to bake for 25 minutes, until puffed, golden and set. WITH ADULT HELP, remove from the oven. Leave to cool for 5 minutes then gently run a round-bladed knife around the inside of each muffin hole. Carefully lift out or tip out onto a serving platter. Serve warm or at room temperature.

Full of flavour and colour, and fragrant spices, this is a mild rather than a hot vegetable chilli, made with butter beans and kidney beans, plus plenty of vegetables.

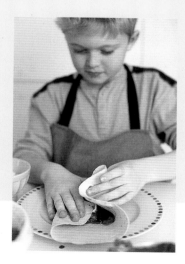

vegetable chilli

Serves 4–6

1 medium red onion
1 medium aubergine
1 red pepper
1 green pepper
2 tablespoons olive oil
2 teaspoons mild chilli powder
2 teaspoons ground cumin
2 teaspoons ground coriander
1 teaspoon dried oregano
salt and freshly ground black
   pepper
2 x 400 g cans chopped
   tomatoes
1 x 410 g can red kidney
   beans in water
1 x 410 g can butter beans
   in water

To serve:
a few sprigs of fresh coriander
a small tub of sour cream
cooked rice or flour tortillas

a large flameproof, ovenproof
*   casserole with lid*

1 ASK AN ADULT TO HELP YOU preheat the oven to 180°C (350°F) Gas 4.

2 Peel the onion to remove the papery outer skin. WITH ADULT HELP, using a small sharp knife, cut the onion in half from top to bottom. Set the halves on the cutting board flat side down and carefully cut into thin slices. Put on one side.

3 Rinse the aubergine and both peppers under the cold tap and drain. Trim the ends off the aubergine then carefully slice it in half from top to bottom. Set the halves on the cutting board cut or flat-side down. Cut each half into 5 long thin strips from top to bottom then cut these strips across every 1 cm. Set aside.

4 Cut the stalks off the peppers, then slice the peppers in half from top to bottom and pull out the cores and seeds. Cut the peppers into pieces about the same size as the aubergine.

5 Spoon the olive oil into the casserole. ASK AN ADULT TO HELP YOU put the casserole on the stove and heat gently. Add the onions to the casserole and stir with a wooden spoon. Cook gently for 10 minutes until the onions are softened. Spoon the chilli powder, cumin,

coriander, oregano and a little salt and black pepper into the casserole and stir well. Cook gently for 2 minutes, then stir again. Put the aubergines into the casserole and stir until they are coated in the onion and spice mix. Add the peppers and stir just to mix.

6 ASK AN ADULT TO HELP YOU carefully open the cans of tomatoes and add to the casserole, then stir well. Open the cans of beans and drain thoroughly in a colander.

7 Stir the beans into the casserole. It might seem that there's a lot, but the vegetables will cook down and release their juices.

8 Cover with the lid and ASK AN ADULT TO HELP YOU put the casserole in the preheated oven to bake for 1 hour. ASK AN ADULT TO HELP YOU carefully remove the casserole from the oven, remove the lid and stir gently. Taste and add more salt and pepper (or chilli) if you think it needs some. Decorate with fresh coriander sprigs and serve with sour cream, plus rice or warm flour tortillas.

pizza and calzone

Makes 4 pizzas or calzones

For the dough:
400 g strong white bread flour
1 teaspoon salt
1 x 7 g sachet easy-blend
(fast-action) dried yeast
1 teaspoon dried mixed herbs
250 ml lukewarm water
1 tablespoon olive oil

For the topping or filling:
200 g cherry tomatoes
1 small red pepper
1 x 150 g tub mini mozzarella
cheese balls
2 tablespoons olive oil
2 garlic cloves
a small bunch of fresh basil
freshly ground black pepper
2 tablespoons pitted olives
thin-sliced salami or chorizo,
anchovies or sweetcorn

2 non-stick baking trays,
greased or 4 metal
pizza trays

1 Make the dough first: put the flour, salt, dried yeast and dried herbs in a mixing bowl and mix well with your hand. Make a well in the dough, then pour the lukewarm water and oil into the well. Gradually work the flour into the liquids to make a soft dough. Flours vary so if there are dry crumbs in the bowl or the dough feels stiff and dry add more water, 1 tablespoon at a time. If the dough is very sticky and clings to your fingers or the bowl, work in a little more flour. Sprinkle a little flour onto the work surface and tip the dough out onto it. Now knead the dough by stretching it away from you then gathering it back into a ball. Do this for 5–10 minutes until the dough feels really smooth and elastic. The dough can also be mixed and kneaded using a large electric mixer fitted with a dough hook. ASK AN ADULT TO HELP YOU mix the dough on low speed and then knead it for 2–5 minutes.

2 Return the dough to the mixing bowl and cover the bowl with a snap-on lid or slip the bowl into a large clean plastic bag, then put the bowl in a warm place for the dough to rise until doubled in size – this will take about 1 hour.

3 ASK AN ADULT TO HELP YOU preheat the oven to 200°C (400°F) Gas 6. Uncover the risen dough and punch it down with your fist to deflate it. Flour the work surface again and tip the dough out onto it. Divide the dough into four equal portions. Using your floured fingers or a rolling pin, press, pull or roll out each piece of dough to a fairly thin circle about 22 cm across. Leave to rest while you make the filling or topping.

4 Rinse the cherry tomatoes and pepper. Cut each tomato in half. Cut the pepper in half and carefully cut away the core with its seeds, and the stem, then cut the pepper into strips. Leave tiny cocktail-sized balls of cheese whole but if using a large ball thinly slice it or pull it into shreds using your fingers.

5 Pour the olive oil into a small bowl. Peel and crush the garlic and add it to the oil. Snip the basil leaves with kitchen scissors and stir in with plenty of black pepper.

6 To assemble: put a teaspoon or so of the oil mixture onto each circle of dough and spread evenly over the dough.

Homemade pizzas taste so good, and they are less greasy than most ready-made ones. A calzone is a type of pizza that's folded with a filling and it's a lot of fun to make!

7 For pizzas: arrange the circles of dough on the prepared baking trays or metal pizza trays then arrange the tomatoes cut-side up on the circles of dough, leaving a 2 cm border of dough all around the edges. Top with the strips of pepper, cheese and olives, plus any of the extra toppings that you want to use.

8 For calzone: arrange the tomatoes cut-side up on one half of each circle of dough leaving a 2 cm border of dough all around. Top with the strips of pepper and the cheese, then the olives. Add any of the extra toppings that you like. Brush the edges of the dough with a little water then fold the dough over the filling to cover it. Press and pinch the edges together with your fingers to firmly seal in the filling. Put the calzones on the prepared baking trays.

9 ASK AN ADULT TO HELP YOU put your pizzas or calzones in the preheated oven to bake. This will take 15–20 minutes for the pizzas and 25 minutes for the calzones. The calzone is ready when it is a golden brown colour. When your pizzas or calzones are ready, ASK AN ADULT TO HELP YOU remove them from the oven and leave to cool for a few minutes before eating. Take care when you eat your calzones as the filling will be very hot!

Risotto is usually made on top of the stove, with hot liquid gradually being stirred into the rice. I have cheated in this recipe as all the ingredients are cooked together in the oven, but the result is a very easy and tasty one-pot meal.

oven risotto with tomatoes, peas & tuna

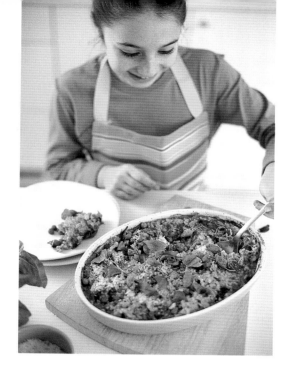

Serves 4–5

4 spring onions

2 garlic cloves

2 x 185 g cans tuna in oil or spring water

2 tablespoons olive oil

200 g Arborio rice (Italian risotto rice)

1 x 400 g can chopped tomatoes with herbs

400 ml hot vegetable stock

100 g fresh or frozen peas (no need to thaw if frozen)

salt and freshly ground black pepper

3 tablespoons freshly grated Parmesan cheese

a few fresh basil leaves, to garnish

a medium-sized heavy flameproof, ovenproof casserole with lid

1 ASK AN ADULT TO HELP YOU preheat the oven to 180°C (350°F) Gas 4.

2 ASK AN ADULT TO HELP YOU trim the hairy ends off the spring onions, then trim off the very dark green tops. Rinse the spring onions under the cold tap to get rid of any grit and mud. Using a small sharp knife, cut the spring onions into thin rounds. Peel off the papery skins from the garlic, then crush or finely chop the cloves. Carefully open the cans of tuna and drain thoroughly in a colander.

3 Spoon the olive oil into the casserole. Set the casserole on the stove and ASK AN ADULT TO HELP YOU gently heat it. Using a wooden spoon, stir in the spring onions and garlic and cook very gently for 1 minute.

4 Tip the rice into the casserole and stir well. Cook gently for 1 minute then stir in the contents of the can of tomatoes, followed by the stock and tuna. Stir well then add the peas and a little salt and black pepper. Stir once more then cover the casserole. ASK AN ADULT TO HELP YOU put the casserole in the preheated oven to bake for 35 minutes.

5 ASK AN ADULT TO HELP YOU remove the casserole from the oven. Before serving, remove the lid, then scatter over the grated Parmesan cheese and the torn up basil leaves. Eat immediately. This is lovely with a salad made from green leaves and some cherry tomatoes.

Part of the fun of holidays is discovering new foods, and we've had some good crab cakes in Maine, as well as in San Francisco. These are like the ones from our favourite lobster shack on the beach, made with crunchy 'oyster' crackers (the oyster-shaped slightly salted plain crackers served with chowder), and served in a bun with coleslaw on the side. Here the ingredients are mixed together, shaped then baked until golden and crispy. Just add a salad or chips!

oven-baked crunchy crab cakes

Serves 4

450 g white crabmeat (fresh, frozen or canned)
100 g crackers (such as cream crackers)
a small bunch of fresh parsley
1 large free-range egg
2 tablespoons mayonnaise
½ a lemon
½ teaspoon dry mustard
½ teaspoon sweet paprika
a dash of Worcestershire sauce
a dash of Tabasco sauce (optional)
a little salt and freshly ground black pepper

a non-stick baking tray, or large baking dish, greased

1 Drain the crabmeat or thaw it completely, then put it in a large mixing bowl.

2 Smash up the crackers: to do this put them into a plastic bag and smash with a rolling pin to make fine crumbs. Measure out 5 tablespoons of the cracker crumbs and put these into the bowl with the crab. Save the rest of the crumbs for coating the crab cakes.

3 Rinse the parsley under the cold tap and pat dry with kitchen paper. ASK AN ADULT TO HELP YOU chop up the parsley with a sharp knife (or with a herb chopper) and add to the crab. Using a table fork, gently mix the ingredients together.

4 Break the egg into a small bowl and pick out any pieces of shell, then add the mayonnaise. Squeeze the juice from the lemon half with a lemon squeezer. Pour into the bowl with the mayonnaise. Add the mustard, paprika, Worcestershire sauce, Tabasco (if using) and a little salt and pepper and mix together well with a fork.

5 Pour the egg mixture onto the crab mixture and mix thoroughly with a fork.

6 Divide the mixture into 8 equal portions. Using your hands, shape and press each portion into a ball, just like making a snow ball, then pat out the ball to a cake about 7.5 cm across.

7 Put the rest of the cracker crumbs into a shallow dish. Gently dip each crab cake in the crumbs, and scatter some on top, so each cake is lightly coated in crumbs. Set the cakes on the prepared baking tray or dish, slightly apart, then cover with cling film and chill in the fridge for at least 2 hours and up to 6 hours.

8 When ready to cook, ASK AN ADULT TO HELP YOU preheat the oven to 200°C (400°F) Gas 6. Remove the cling film from the crab cakes and ASK AN ADULT TO HELP YOU put them in the preheated oven to bake for 15 minutes, until golden and crispy. ASK AN ADULT TO HELP YOU remove the tray from the oven. Serve your crab cakes hot, with salad, warm rolls and coleslaw.

Make your very own and healthier version of chicken nuggets. Strips of chicken breast are dipped in melted butter then coated in a savoury crumb mixture and baked in the oven. Eat with Thai sweet chilli dipping sauce rather than ketchup, and potato wedges, plus a salad.

oven-fried chicken nuggets with potato wedges

Serves 4

4 medium chicken breasts, skinless and boneless
50 g unsalted butter
100 g fresh breadcrumbs (see tip below)
1 teaspoon sweet paprika
¼ teaspoon dried mixed herbs or *herbes de Provence*
a good pinch of salt
freshly ground black pepper

a large non-stick baking tray or roasting tin, lightly oiled

Potato wedges:
4 medium baking potatoes
4 tablespoons olive oil
a little salt and freshly ground black pepper

a non-stick roasting tin

1 ASK AN ADULT TO HELP YOU preheat the oven to 200°C (400°F) Gas 6. Put the chicken breasts onto a chopping board. ASK AN ADULT TO HELP YOU slice each chicken breast into 5 strips diagonally, using a small sharp knife. Wash your hands then put the butter into a small saucepan and melt gently over low heat.

2 Carefully remove the pan from the heat and put onto a heatproof surface near the chopping board with the chicken strips.

3 Put the breadcrumbs into a large, clean plastic bag. Add the paprika, dried herbs, salt and pepper. Close the bag and shake well to mix.

4 Dip each strip of chicken into the melted butter then put it into the plastic bag with the crumbs. When all the chicken strips are in the bag, close it tightly and shake it well so the chicken gets coated in the crumbs.

5 Remove each chicken strip from the bag and put it on the prepared baking tray, arranging the strips slightly apart and in one layer.

6 ASK AN ADULT TO HELP YOU put the strips in the preheated oven to bake for 15–20 minutes, until a good golden brown and nicely crisp. ASK AN ADULT TO HELP YOU remove the tray from the oven. Use tongs or a fish slice to transfer the chicken to a serving platter and eat immediately.

Tip: To make your own breadcrumbs use sliced bread that is 1 or 2 days old. Carefully cut off the crusts, (you don't need them) then tear each slice of bread into about 8 pieces. ASK AN ADULT TO HELP YOU put them in a food processor or blender and process to make fine crumbs.

Potato wedges

1 ASK AN ADULT TO HELP YOU preheat the oven to 200°C (400°F) Gas 6. Wash the potatoes under the cold tap, scrubbing lightly with a vegetable brush to get rid of any earth. Pat dry with kitchen paper.

2 Put the potatoes on a chopping board. ASK AN ADULT TO HELP YOU carefully cut each potato in half lengthways, using a sharp knife. Cut each half into 3 long wedges.

3 Put the wedges into the roasting tin. Spoon over the oil, and sprinkle with salt and pepper. Using your hands, gently toss the wedges so they get coated in the oil. Put them skin-side down in the tin.

4 ASK AN ADULT TO HELP YOU put the wedges in the preheated oven to bake for about 1 hour, until a good brown. ASK AN ADULT TO HELP YOU remove the tin from the oven, and transfer the potato wedges to a serving dish. Eat them while they are still hot.

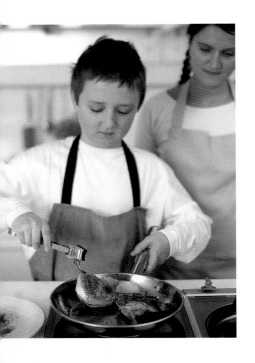

My son Dan's grandparents introduced him to *confit de canard* one Easter in Paris. When he returned he wanted to know how it was made so we could enjoy it without making a trip to France. Luckily it's very simple. Confit is the French way of preserving meat by lightly salting it and then gently cooking it in plenty of fat. It is then kept in the fat (in the fridge these days) until ready to serve. The legs are then quickly cooked until very hot and crispy and eaten with potatoes or with lentils or white beans, and a green salad. Don't forget to wash your hands really well after you have been touching the duck legs.

dan's duck confit

Serves 4

4 duck legs
1 tablespoon sea salt or
    coarse salt
½ teaspoon coarsely ground
    black pepper
3 sprigs of fresh thyme
2 bay leaves
340 g can goose fat or 350 g
    pack of lard

a heavy flameproof,
*   ovenproof casserole with*
*   a lid*

1 You'll need a casserole with a lid that will take the legs in a single layer, even if they are squashed together.

2 Wipe the duck legs with kitchen paper and put in a large mixing bowl. Mix the salt and pepper and rub all over each leg, on the skin side and the underside, and in all the nooks and crannies. Cover the bowl with cling film and put into the fridge for 2–3 hours.

3 Uncover the legs and wipe them, one at a time, with kitchen paper to remove as much of the salt as possible. As you finish each leg put it into the casserole skin-side down. The legs should be in a single layer but can slightly overlap and it's fine to squash them together. Scatter the thyme sprigs and bay leaves on top.

4 ASK AN ADULT TO HELP YOU preheat the oven to 150°C (300°F) Gas 2.

5 Set the casserole on top of the stove and ASK AN ADULT TO HELP YOU turn on the heat to low. Leave the casserole to heat up gently and to melt some of the fat on the duck legs. After about 10 minutes there should be a puddle of fat around the legs, if not, cook for 5 minutes longer. Turn off the heat and spoon the goose fat or lard over the legs. Cover the casserole with the lid then ASK AN ADULT TO HELP YOU put the confit in the preheated oven to bake for 2 hours, without opening the oven door if possible.

6 ASK AN ADULT TO remove the casserole from the oven – it is full of hot fat so you must be very careful! Leave it to cool on a heatproof surface. When completely cold, transfer the casserole to the fridge and leave for at least 1 day and up to 4 days for the flavours to develop.

7 To eat the duck, take the casserole out of the fridge and leave it at room temperature for a few hours to soften the fat. Carefully remove the legs from the fat, scraping off as much fat as possible with a round-bladed table knife.

8 Put the legs skin-side down in a cold non-stick frying pan. Put the pan over low to medium heat. The legs sometimes splutter and spit so ASK AN ADULT TO HELP YOU cook the confit gently for about 10 minutes, until the skin is

crispy and brown. Carefully turn the legs over and cook the other side for 5–7 minutes until lightly browned.

9 Eat warm from the pan, or keep warm in a low oven while, WITH ADULT HELP, you fry some sliced cooked potatoes in the fat in the pan. Save the fat left from the casserole to make another batch of confit or use it for roasting potatoes.

Lean minced lamb mixed with mild, aromatic Middle Eastern spices is pressed onto skewers and baked until browned then eaten with pita breads and a simple yoghurt dip. Add a couple of simple salads like sliced tomato, and grated carrot mixed with a little fresh lemon juice, seasoning and sesame seeds.

lamb koftas with pita pockets

Serves 4

500 g lean minced lamb
1 small red onion
2 teaspoons mild paprika
1½ teaspoons ground
**   coriander**
1½ teaspoons ground cumin
¼ teaspoon ground cinnamon
4 grinds of freshly ground
**   black pepper**
a good pinch of salt
a few sprigs of fresh flat leaf
**   parsley or coriander**

For the dip:
200 ml natural yoghurt
a good pinch of salt
freshly ground black pepper
a small bunch of chives
a few sprigs fresh flat leaf
**   parsley or coriander**
8 small or picnic-sized pitas,
**   to serve**

16 wooden skewers
a baking tray or roasting tin,
*   lined with foil and oiled*

1 ASK AN ADULT TO HELP YOU preheat the oven to 220°C (425°F) Gas 7. Soak the skewers in a bowl of water (this stops the wood from burning in the oven). Meanwhile, make up the meat mix.

2 Tip the minced lamb into a large mixing bowl. Peel the skin away from the onion and throw it away. Carefully grate the onion onto the lamb using the coarse or large hole side of a grater.

3 Measure the spices – paprika, ground coriander, ground cumin, ground cinnamon, black pepper – and salt into the bowl. Using kitchen scissors, snip the parsley or coriander sprigs into the bowl. Put your hands into the bowl and mix together all the ingredients, squeezing it between your fingers until it looks evenly mixed. (If you have plenty of time you can now cover the bowl and chill it in the fridge for up to 5 hours before finishing the recipe.)

4 Divide the meat mixture into 16 even portions. Using your hands, mould each portion of meat around a skewer to make an egg or sausage shape about 10 cm long. Arrange the skewers on the prepared baking tray. Wash your hands thoroughly.

5 ASK AN ADULT TO HELP YOU put the baking tray in the preheated oven and bake the koftas for 15 minutes, until well-browned.

6 While the meat is cooking, make the dip by mixing the yoghurt with the salt and pepper. Snip the chives and parsley or coriander into small pieces with kitchen scissors and mix into the yoghurt. Spoon into a serving bowl.

7 When the koftas are ready, ASK AN ADULT TO HELP YOU lift the tray out of the oven. Transfer the skewers to a serving plate and serve with the yoghurt dip and warm pitas.

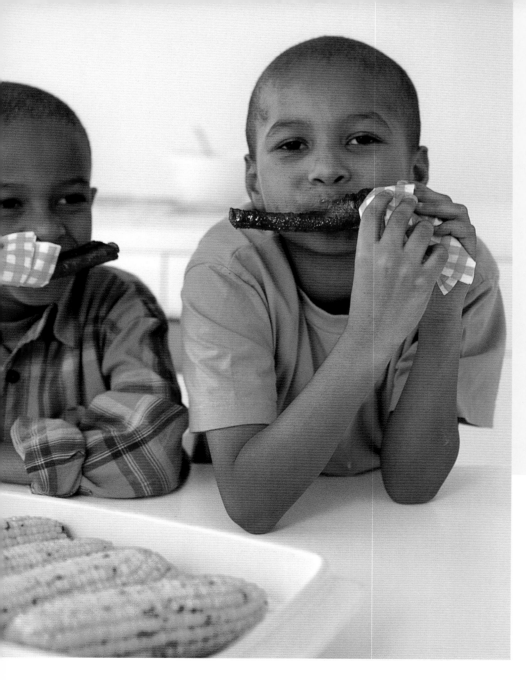

For this recipe you need good meaty spareribs or king ribs. For a filling supper, cook some large baking potatoes in the oven at the same time as you cook the ribs. You could also roast some sweetcorn to complete the meal or make a big green salad.

sticky maple ribs with roast sweetcorn

Serves 4

1 medium red onion
3 tablespoons maple syrup
3 tablespoons soy sauce
3 tablespoons tomato ketchup
1½ tablespoons mild mustard
1½ tablespoons
  Worcestershire sauce
freshly ground black pepper
1.2 kg spareribs

a large, non-stick roasting tin

Easy roast corn:
4 fresh corn-on-the-cobs
75 g unsalted butter
a little freshly ground black
  pepper

*an ovenproof dish, large
  enough to take the
  sweetcorn in a single layer*

1 ASK AN ADULT TO HELP YOU preheat the oven to 190°C (375°F) Gas 5.

2 Add a little oil to the roasting tin and rub it around the inside with a piece of kitchen paper.

3 Peel the skin away from the onion and throw it away. Grate the onion into a large mixing bowl using the coarse or large hole side of a grater.

4 Add the maple syrup, soy sauce, tomato ketchup, mustard, Worcestershire sauce and 4 grinds of black pepper. Mix together well.

5 Add the ribs to the bowl one at a time and use a metal spoon to thoroughly cover the ribs with the sticky glaze. Carefully lift the ribs into the prepared tin. Wash your hands thoroughly before doing anything else.

6 ASK AN ADULT TO HELP YOU put the roasting tin in the preheated oven. Bake for 30 minutes then ASK AN ADULT TO HELP YOU remove the tin from the oven. Using kitchen tongs, carefully turn over the ribs so they brown evenly.

7 ASK AN ADULT TO HELP YOU put the tin back in the oven and bake for another 30 minutes.

8 The ribs should be a dark golden brown and crispy around the edges. ASK AN ADULT TO HELP YOU lift the tin out of the oven. Carefully transfer the ribs to a serving plate and eat!

Easy roast corn

1 ASK AN ADULT TO HELP YOU preheat the oven to 190°C (375°F) Gas 5.

2 If the corn still has its green leafy covering it must be 'shucked' – pull off the leaves from the top pointy end, then pull off all the silky hairs.

3 ASK AN ADULT TO HELP YOU melt the butter: either put it in a small saucepan over the lowest possible heat, or microwave it in a bowl on medium for about 20 seconds.

4 Pour the butter into the baking dish, add a little black pepper then put the corn into the dish and turn them so they are well coated in butter.

5 ASK AN ADULT TO HELP YOU put the dish in the preheated oven to bake for 30 minutes. ASK AN ADULT TO HELP YOU turn the corn over twice during this time – cooking tongs work best for this. Leave to cool slightly before eating.

puddings

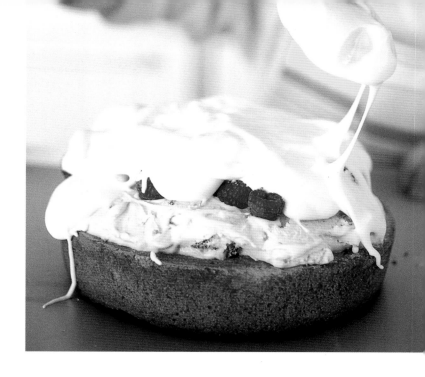

baked alaska

Makes 1 large cake

For the sponge:
115 g plain flour
1 teaspoon baking powder
115 g caster sugar
115 g unsalted butter, very
soft
½ teaspoon vanilla essence
2 large free-range eggs
1 tablespoon milk

To finish:
500 ml strawberry, raspberry
or vanilla ice cream
4 egg whites
230 g caster sugar
150 g raspberries
icing sugar, for sprinkling

a sandwich cake tin or
springform cake tin, 21 cm
diameter
greaseproof paper
a baking tray

1 ASK AN ADULT TO HELP YOU preheat the oven to 180°C (350°F) Gas 4. Put a little soft butter on a piece of kitchen paper and rub it around the inside of the tin. Put the tin on the greaseproof paper and draw around it. Cut just inside the line to make a disc of paper. Fit this into the base of the tin. Put to one side.

2 Sift the flour and baking powder into a mixing bowl. Stir in the sugar. Add the very soft butter and vanilla essence to the bowl.

3 Break the eggs into a small bowl. Pick out any pieces of shell then lightly beat the eggs and the milk with a fork to break them up. Pour the eggs into the mixing bowl. Beat all the ingredients with a wooden spoon, or ASK AN ADULT TO HELP YOU use an electric mixer or whisk, until the mixture is very smooth and light. Spoon the cake mixture into the prepared tin and spread it around evenly.

4 ASK AN ADULT TO HELP YOU put the sponge cake in the preheated oven to bake for about 25 minutes, until a light golden brown. To test if the cake is cooked, ASK AN ADULT TO HELP YOU remove it from the oven and gently press it in the middle. If it springs back it is cooked, if there is a dimple then bake for 5 minutes more. ASK AN ADULT TO HELP YOU remove the sponge from the oven, leave for 2 minutes, then run a round-bladed knife around the inside of the tin and carefully turn out the cake onto a wire rack and leave to cool completely. Turn off the oven.

5 Remove the ice cream from the freezer and leave until soft enough to spoon onto the sponge; put the sponge cake onto a baking tray, then scoop or spoon the ice cream on top to make an even layer. Put the whole thing back into the freezer and leave until very firm – at least 1 hour, but you can leave it in the freezer for up to 3 days.

This is great fun to make and eat! You can use a ready-made sponge flan case or cake for the base, and choose your favourite flavour of ice cream. It's good served with a sauce made from ripe strawberries mashed using a fork or a blender, mixed with a little bit of icing sugar.

6 When you are ready to finish the alaska, ASK AN ADULT TO HELP YOU preheat the oven to 220°C (425°F) Gas 7. Put the egg whites into a very clean mixing bowl. Stand the bowl on a damp cloth to keep it from wobbling. Using a rotary, or electric mixer or hand whisk, whisk until the whites turn into a stiff white foam – lift out the whisk and there will be a little peak of white standing on the end.

7 Quickly whisk the caster sugar into the egg whites to make a stiff and glossy meringue.

8 Remove the sponge and ice cream from the freezer. Arrange the raspberries on top of the ice cream. Quickly cover the whole thing with the meringue, spreading it evenly. Make sure that there are no holes or gaps and the meringue covers every single millimetre of the cake and ice cream. Sprinkle with sifted icing sugar.

9 ASK AN ADULT TO HELP YOU put the alaska in the preheated oven to bake for just 4–5 minutes, until lightly browned. Serve immediately.

At first glance this fun dessert looks like a nutty meringue, but hidden underneath is an apple stuffed with apricots! Eat it with a scoop of vanilla ice cream.

apple hedgehogs

Makes 4 hedgehogs

4 small to medium Bramley cooking apples, or large tart eating apples
8 ready-to-eat dried apricots
3 egg whites
150 g caster sugar
4 tablespoons flaked almonds

a large shallow ovenproof baking dish

1 ASK AN ADULT TO HELP YOU preheat the oven to 180°C (350°F) Gas 4. Put a small amount of soft butter on a piece of kitchen paper and rub it around the inside of the baking dish, to grease it

2 Peel the apples with a vegetable peeler then remove the core with an apple corer – ASK AN ADULT TO HELP YOU if this is hard work.

3 Cut the apricots into small pieces with kitchen scissors. Set an apple in each baking dish or arrange them well apart in the large dish. Push the chopped-up apricots into the centre hole in each apple.

4 Put the egg whites into a very clean and dry mixing bowl, or the bowl of an electric mixer. Use a rotary whisk or the whisk attachment of the electric mixer to whisk the egg whites until they are very stiff, and the whisk leaves the mixture in very stiff pointy peaks when you lift it out.

5 Tip in the sugar and whisk again just until all the sugar has been combined. Spoon a quarter of the mixture on top of each apple, then spread the meringue mixture all over the apple to completely cover it. It should look quite rough. Stick the almonds into the meringue to look like the spines on a hedgehog.

6 ASK AN ADULT TO HELP YOU put the apples in the preheated oven to bake for 35 minutes, until a good golden brown.

7 ASK AN ADULT TO HELP YOU carefully remove the apple hedgehogs from the oven then leave them to cool for about 15 minutes before serving.

This is a light, baked cheesecake with lots of fresh raspberries, strawberries and blueberries so it makes a lovely summer dessert. Ricotta is a low-fat soft Italian cheese usually sold in tubs.

lemon ricotta cheesecake with summer berries

Makes 1 large cheesecake

For the crust:
60 g unsalted butter
125 g plain digestive or
   wheaten biscuits
1 tablespoon caster sugar

For the filling:
500 g ricotta cheese
250 ml sour cream
2 large free-range eggs
100 g icing sugar
2 tablespoons ground
   almonds
2 medium unwaxed lemons

For the topping:
2 tablespoons flaked almonds
fresh summer berries, to serve

*a springform cake tin or deep
   flan tin, 22 cm diameter*

1 ASK AN ADULT TO HELP YOU preheat the oven to 150°C (300°F) Gas 2.

2 Lightly rub the inside of the tin with a little soft butter on a piece of kitchen paper.

3 ASK AN ADULT TO HELP YOU melt the butter for the crust: put the butter in a small saucepan and melt on the stove over low heat, or if you like, you can melt the butter in the microwave.

4 Put the biscuits in a plastic bag. Make sure the ends of the bag are tightly closed then crush the biscuits into crumbs by hitting them with a rolling pin. Tip the crumbs into a mixing bowl and add the melted butter and the sugar. Mix well with a wooden spoon then tip the mixture into the tin.

5 Roughly spread the crumbs in the tin so they are evenly distributed then, using the back of a metal spoon, press the crumbs onto the base of the tin to make an even layer. Put the tin in the fridge to chill while you make the filling.

6 Put the ricotta and sour cream into a large mixing bowl or the bowl of a food processor. Break the eggs into the bowl, remove any pieces of shell, then add the icing sugar and ground almonds.

7 Rinse the lemons then grate the yellow zest straight into the bowl using a lemon zester or a fine grater. Cut the lemons in half and squeeze out the juice with a lemon squeezer. Pour the juice into the bowl.

8 Mix all the ingredients together using a wooden spoon until completely smooth. ASK AN ADULT TO HELP YOU blend the ingredients in a food processor or if you want to use an electric mixer (use slow speed).

9 Pour the filling carefully into the tin then scatter the flaked almonds on the top.

10 ASK AN ADULT TO HELP YOU put the tin in the preheated oven. Bake for 1¼ hours then turn off the oven and leave the cheesecake inside (don't open the door) to cool slowly as the oven cools down. After 1½ hours, remove it from the oven. If you have used a springform tin, gently remove the cheesecake from the tin.

11 Store your cheesecake in an airtight container in the fridge and eat it within 3 days. For the best flavour, remove it from the fridge about 30 minutes before eating. Serve the cheesecake either topped with or surrounded by the berries or put them in a separate bowl so everyone can help themselves.

chocolate & coconut rice pudding

Serves 4–6

50 g pudding rice or Arborio rice (Italian risotto rice)
3 tablespoons caster sugar
a 400 g can coconut milk or 400 ml whole milk
500 ml milk
50 g plain chocolate

an ovenproof baking dish, about 1 litre capacity, buttered

1 ASK AN ADULT TO HELP YOU preheat the oven to 150°C (300°F) Gas 2.

2 Put the rice and sugar in the prepared baking dish. Pour the coconut milk and milk into the dish and stir gently.

3 ASK AN ADULT TO HELP YOU put the pudding in the preheated oven to bake for 2 hours, then WITH ADULT HELP carefully take the pudding out of the oven. Stir it very gently with a wooden spoon to break up the skin and mix well.

4 Break up the chocolate and scatter the pieces over the pudding. Stir just to marble the chocolate through the pudding.

5 ASK AN ADULT TO HELP YOU put the pudding back in the oven and bake it for another 30 minutes. WITH ADULT HELP, carefully remove the pudding from the oven and let cool for 20–30 minutes before eating.

Coconut and toffee pudding: make the pudding as above and bake it for 2 hours. ASK AN ADULT TO HELP YOU remove it from the oven but do not stir. Sprinkle 60 g dark brown muscovado sugar or molasses sugar (instead of chocolate) over the surface. Return to the oven and bake for a further 30 minutes. WITH ADULT HELP, remove it from the oven and let it cool for 30 minutes before serving.

An easy-to-make rice pudding that's good eaten warm or at room temperature. If you don't like the taste of coconut you can use extra ordinary milk instead.

This is a lovely fruity tart that's just right for eating after a big Sunday lunch as it's not too filling. Serve it with custard or ice cream.

lemon & apple tart

Makes 1 large pie

350 g shortcrust pastry (see note below)

1 large or 2 medium Bramley cooking apples or very tart baking apples, about 300 g

3 rounded tablespoons golden syrup

50 g fresh bread, without crusts

1 large unwaxed lemon

a shallow pie plate or tart tin, 26 cm diameter

1 ASK AN ADULT TO HELP YOU preheat the oven to 190°C (375°F) Gas 5. Sprinkle a little flour on your work surface, then gently roll out the pastry (using a rolling pin sprinkled with flour) to a circle the same size as your pie plate. Roll the pastry round the rolling pin then lift it over the plate so the pastry drapes over it. Carefully press the pastry onto the base, making sure you have pressed out any pockets of air. Finally, press the pastry onto the rim.

2 With kitchen scissors, carefully snip off any excess pastry that is hanging over the edge of the plate (you can save this to make some decorations). Decorate the rim of the tart by pressing the pastry with the prongs of a fork to make a stripy pattern. Put the pie plate in the fridge to chill while you make the filling.

3 Peel the apples with a vegetable peeler, then remove the core with an apple corer or ASK AN ADULT TO HELP YOU cut the apple into quarters, then cut out the core. Grate the apple into a mixing bowl. Add the golden syrup to the bowl.

4 Break up the bread and put it in a food processor or blender. ASK AN ADULT TO HELP YOU process it to make fine crumbs. Tip the crumbs into the bowl with the apple. Rinse the lemon under the tap and pat dry. Grate the yellow zest straight into the mixing bowl using a lemon zester or fine grater. Cut the lemon in half and squeeze out the juice with a lemon squeezer. Pour the juice into the bowl with the other ingredients.

5 Mix all the ingredients really well using a table fork in each hand to stir and toss everything together. Gently spoon the filling onto the pastry base – don't press the filling or it might lose its fluffy texture. You can decorate the tart with pastry scraps cut into shapes using fancy cutters or pastry strips to make a lattice pattern on top.

6 ASK AN ADULT TO HELP YOU put the tart in the preheated oven to bake for 30 minutes, until golden. ASK AN ADULT TO HELP YOU remove it from the oven and eat warm or at room temperature with yoghurt or ice cream. Your tart is best eaten within 2 days of baking.

Shortcrust pastry: you can use ready-made fresh or frozen pastry (defrost according to the packet instructions). Some brands make sheets of ready-rolled pastry. To make your own, put 225 g plain flour and a pinch of salt into the bowl of a food processor. Add 160 g unsalted butter (straight from the fridge), cut into small pieces. ASK AN ADULT TO HELP YOU process it until the mixture makes fine crumbs. Add 2 tablespoons of icy cold water and process again until the dough comes together in a ball.

The appeal of this fruit tart is its rustic, homemade charm. This is nothing like a tart from a fancy patisserie! Use slightly underripe peaches, pears or dessert apples, and you can add nuts, raisins or sultanas and a little cinnamon when you mix in the caster sugar.

free-form peach pie

Makes 1 large pie

For the pastry:
225 g plain flour
a good pinch of salt
a good pinch of ground
**   cinnamon**
2 tablespoons caster sugar
150 g unsalted butter, straight
**   from the fridge**
3 tablespoons cold water

For the filling:
5 medium peaches, about
**   750 g, or eating apples**
**   or pears**
3 tablespoons caster sugar,
**   plus extra for sprinkling**

a large baking tray
a sheet of non-stick baking
*   parchment*

1 First make the pastry using the food processor: put the flour, salt, cinnamon and sugar into the bowl of the processor. ASK AN ADULT TO HELP YOU run the machine for a few seconds just to combine all the ingredients.

2 Cut the butter into small pieces and add to the bowl of the processor and ASK AN ADULT TO HELP YOU run the machine until the ingredients look like coarse crumbs. Pour in the water through the feed tube and run the machine until the dough comes together in a ball.

3 Sprinkle a little flour over your work surface. WITH ADULT HELP, carefully remove the dough from the processor. Put the dough onto the work surface and gently knead and work the dough for a few seconds until the dough looks smooth.

4 Put the sheet of non-stick baking parchment onto the work surface. Put the ball of dough in the middle of the paper. Sprinkle a rolling pin with flour and gently roll out the dough to a circle about 30 cm across. Slide the sheet of paper with the dough on it onto the baking tray and chill in the fridge for 15 minutes while you make the filling.

5 ASK AN ADULT TO HELP YOU preheat the oven to 200°C (400°F) Gas 6. Rinse the fruit under the cold tap and pat dry. WITH ADULT HELP, slice the peaches in half along the line that runs from the stem down to the base. Twist the peach so the two halves separate. Pull the halves apart and remove the stone. Cut each half into 4 thick slices. If using apples, peel them only if the skin is tough. Quarter them, cut out the cores and slice thickly. Peel the pears with a potato peeler, quarter them, cut out the cores and slice thickly.

6 Sprinkle the sliced fruit with the 3 tablespoons sugar, and mix gently. Remove the dough from the fridge. Heap the sliced fruit into the centre of the dough, mounding it evenly. Leave a wide border of pastry, about 9 cm, without fruit.

7 Gently fold the border of pastry over the fruit so the fruit in the centre is uncovered, leaving a gap of about 2 cm between the fruit and the fold, and gently pinch the folds or pleats of pastry together every 6 cm. Try not to press the dough down onto the fruit.

8 Using a pastry brush, lightly brush the pastry with cold water then sprinkle with caster sugar.

9 ASK AN ADULT TO HELP YOU put the pie in the preheated oven to bake for 40 minutes, until golden brown. ASK AN ADULT TO HELP YOU remove it from the oven and leave to cool on its tray for 10 minutes. Slide the tart off its paper lining and onto a serving platter while it is still warm, and serve.

Another family holiday favourite, this time from France. A clafoutis is a dessert made from fresh cherries baked in a rich custardy topping. I've added blueberries and blackberries to my own recipe, but you can also use pears (peeled, cored and diced) or sliced fresh apricots.

cherry & berry clafoutis

Makes 1 large clafoutis

150 g blueberries
150 g blackberries
200 g cherries
2 large free-range eggs
250 g crème fraiche or double cream
100 g caster sugar, plus extra for sprinkling
2 tablespoons plain flour
½ teaspoon vanilla essence

a shallow ovenproof dish about 1.5 litre capacity, greased

1 ASK AN ADULT TO HELP YOU preheat the oven to 180°C (350°F) Gas 4.

2 Rinse the blueberries and blackberries in a colander under the cold tap. Drain thoroughly then put them in the prepared baking dish.

3 Rinse the cherries then ASK AN ADULT TO HELP YOU remove the stones with a cherry stoner. Put them on top of the berries.

4 Break the eggs into a mixing bowl and pick out any pieces of shell. Add the crème fraiche or cream, sugar, flour and vanilla essence to the mixing bowl. Beat gently with a balloon whisk, rotary whisk or fork until thoroughly mixed.

5 Carefully pour the egg mixture over the fruit. Sprinkle with a little extra sugar then ASK AN ADULT TO HELP YOU put the clafoutis into the preheated oven to bake for about 35 minutes, until golden and just set when you gently wobble the dish.

6 ASK AN ADULT TO HELP YOU remove the dish from the oven, leave it for 15 minutes on a heatproof surface and then eat it while it is still warm with a scoop of vanilla ice cream.

On holiday in Vermont we visited a bakery and this maple pie was a big hit! Early each spring the maple trees there are tapped to produce the sap, which is boiled down to make syrup. It takes 40 gallons of sap to make just one gallon of the wonderful syrup!

maple pie

Makes 1 large pie

For the pastry:
300 g plain flour
a pinch of salt
200 g unsalted butter, straight from the fridge
3 tablespoons icy cold water
or
500 g ready-made shortcrust pastry, defrosted if necessary

For the filling:
2 large free-range eggs
275 ml maple syrup
150 ml double cream
2 tablespoons plain flour
100 g walnut pieces
icing sugar or maple sugar, for sprinkling

a deep flan case or pie dish, 23 cm diameter
a baking tray
non-stick baking parchment
shaped pastry cutters

1 First make the pastry, unless you are using the ready-made pastry. Put the flour and salt into the bowl of a food processor. Cut the butter into small chunks and add to the bowl. ASK AN ADULT TO HELP YOU run the machine until the mixture looks like fine crumbs. Pour in the cold water through the feed tube and run the machine until the crumbs come together to make a firm dough. ASK AN ADULT TO HELP YOU remove the dough from the bowl.

2 Scatter a little flour over the work surface. Put the dough or ready-made pastry on the floured surface and gently roll out with a rolling pin to a large circle 36 cm across. Roll the circle around the rolling pin and lift it over the flan tin or pie dish. Gently unroll the dough so it drapes over the tin. Carefully press the dough onto the bottom of the tin and up the sides so there are no bubbles of air. Roll the pin over the top of the flan case to cut off the overhanging dough (or snip it off with kitchen scissors). Save the pastry for the decorations. Gently use your thumbs to press the pastry sides upwards so the pastry stands about 5 cm higher than the rim of the tin. Prick the base a few times with a fork, then chill in the fridge for 20 minutes.

3 ASK AN ADULT TO HELP YOU preheat the oven to 200°C (400°F) Gas 6. Take the chilled pastry in its flan tin out of the fridge. Cut a round of non-stick baking parchment 36 cm across. Crumple the paper to make it soft then open it out and gently press it into the pastry case to cover the base and sides. Fill the case with baking beans, dried beans or uncooked rice to weigh the paper down. ASK AN ADULT TO HELP YOU put it in the preheated oven to bake for 15 minutes. ASK AN ADULT TO HELP YOU remove the pastry case from the oven and carefully remove the paper and beans. Turn the oven down to 190°C (375°F) Gas 5 and bake the pastry case for 5 minutes more, until a light gold colour. Put a baking tray into the oven to heat up.

4 To make the filling break the eggs into a mixing bowl or large jug. Pick out any pieces of shell. Add the maple syrup, cream and flour and mix well with a rotary whisk until smooth.

5 ASK AN ADULT TO HELP YOU remove the pastry case from the oven. Stand the pastry case in its flan tin on the hot baking tray. Scatter the walnuts over the base of the pastry case. Carefully pour the filling over the nuts then ASK AN ADULT TO HELP YOU put it in the oven to bake for 30 minutes, until lightly coloured.

6 Roll out the leftover pastry fairly thinly and cut into shapes using fancy cutters (maple leaves or whatever you like). ASK AN ADULT TO HELP YOU remove the pie from the oven and gently arrange the pastry shapes on top. Return the pie to the oven and bake for 10 minutes more. WITH ADULT HELP, carefully remove it from the oven and leave to cool. Eat while still warm. Sprinkle with icing sugar or maple sugar before serving.

These are rich but light puddings, made without flour. If you don't want to use nuts, you can replace the ground almonds with 2 tablespoons of plain flour. Eat warm from the oven, topped with a scoop of vanilla or white chocolate ice cream. Yum!

warm chocolate puddings

Makes 6 small puddings

150 g good plain chocolate
100 g unsalted butter
2 large free-range eggs,
   at room temperature
2 egg yolks, at room
   temperature
5 tablespoons caster sugar
2 tablespoons ground
   almonds

6 x 150 ml ramekins or similar ovenproof dishes
a baking tray

1 ASK AN ADULT TO HELP YOU preheat the oven to 220°C (425°F) Gas 7. Put a little soft butter on a piece of kitchen paper and rub inside the ramekins, then set the ramekins on a baking tray.

2 Break up the chocolate and put it in a heatproof mixing bowl. Cut up the butter into chunks and add to the bowl.

3 Half fill a medium saucepan with water and WITH ADULT HELP put it on the stove and heat until the water boils. Turn off the heat and carefully set the mixing bowl containing the chocolate and butter over the hot water and leave to melt gently.

4 While the chocolate melts, put the 2 whole eggs, the 2 egg yolks and caster sugar into a mixing bowl or the bowl of an electric mixer. Using a rotary whisk or electric whisk or mixer beat the mixture until very light and foamy. Add the ground almonds and whisk for a few seconds.

5 Gently stir the chocolate mixture until smooth. ASK AN ADULT TO HELP YOU remove the bowl from the pan of hot water. Pour the chocolate mixture onto the egg mixture, scrape out the bowl, then whisk until the two mixtures are thoroughly blended.

6 Carefully spoon the chocolate mixture into the prepared ramekins so there is the same amount in each. ASK AN ADULT TO HELP YOU put the baking tray with the ramekins on in the preheated oven to bake for 10 minutes, until slightly puffed and just soft in the middle. ASK AN ADULT TO HELP YOU carefully remove them from the oven and serve them immediately with a scoop of ice cream on top of each pudding.

sticky toffee pudding

Makes 1 large pudding

For the pudding:
175 g stoned chopped dates
300 ml boiling water
1 teaspoon bicarbonate
   of soda
50 g unsalted butter, very soft
175 g caster sugar
½ teaspoon vanilla essence
2 large free-range eggs, at
   room temperature
225 g plain flour
1 teaspoon baking powder

For the sauce:
100 g dark brown muscovado
   sugar
50 g unsalted butter
200 ml single cream

*an ovenproof baking dish,
   about 1.5 litre capacity,
   greased*

1 ASK AN ADULT TO HELP YOU preheat the oven to 180°C (350°F) Gas 4.

2 Put the dates in a small saucepan or heatproof bowl. ASK AN ADULT TO HELP YOU pour over the boiling water then stir in the bicarbonate of soda and leave to soak until needed.

3 Put the very soft butter in a mixing bowl or the bowl of an electric mixer. Add the caster sugar and the vanilla essence and beat with a wooden spoon or electric whisk (WITH ADULT HELP) until very well combined (the mixture won't look soft and fluffy like a sponge cake mix).

4 Break the eggs into a bowl or small jug, pick out any pieces of shell then beat with a fork just to break up the eggs. Pour a little of the egg mix into the mixing bowl and beat well. Keep on adding the eggs, a little at a time, then beating well, until all the eggs have been used up.

5 Set a sieve over the bowl and tip the flour and baking powder into the sieve and sift into the bowl. Stir gently a few times to half-mix in the flour, then pour the date and water mixture into the bowl. Carefully mix the whole lot together to make a runny batter.

6 Pour the pudding batter into the prepared dish. ASK AN ADULT TO HELP YOU put the pudding in the preheated oven to bake for about 40–45 minutes, until a good golden brown. To test if the pudding is cooked, ASK AN ADULT TO HELP YOU remove it from the oven and push a cocktail stick into the centre; if the stick comes out clean then the pudding is cooked, if the stick is sticky with mixture then the pudding needs another 5 minutes in the oven, before you test it again.

7 While the pudding is baking, make the sauce. Put the sugar, butter and cream into a small saucepan. ASK AN ADULT TO HELP YOU set the pan over low heat and heat gently, stirring now and then until melted, smooth and hot.

8 ASK AN ADULT TO HELP YOU remove the pudding from the oven. Serve it warm with the hot sauce. Any leftover pudding and sauce can be gently reheated and served again. Eat within 2 days of making.

A really popular sticky pudding from the Lake District of northern England that is just perfect for a cold day. The toffee sauce is also good with ice cream.

index

acknowledgements

The publishers would like to say thank you to all our lovely models, especially Ruby and Savannah, Seren, Max, Phoebe and Yasmin, Davian and Jerrell, Maria, Tabitha, Charlie, Beau and Jake, as well as Molly.

Very special thanks also to Gail Taylor, Amanda Trent, Fiona Sullivan, Kerri Goulty, Elizabeth James, and Sandy of Pregnant Pause Agency.

The publishers would also like to thank Jacqs at Millie Mac for supplying the aprons and oven gloves on the following pages: 2, 6, 9, 16, 17, 22, 23 and 77.

Millie Mac
5 Sunnyside Road
Teddington
Middlesex
TW11 0RP
www.milliemac.co.uk
tel: 020 8977 5779
High quality and hand made range of children's and adults products from oven gloves and aprons to bags and bibs.